Become

A Master of

Closing Sales

All Rights Reserved by

Vibhor Asri Publishing

ISBN: 978-93-5659-574-3

Copyright © VIBHOR ASRI

Become A Master of Closing Sales

The Ultimate Course on Closing Deals

Vibhor Asri

www.vibhorasri.com

All our course materials are protected by copyright laws. Materials may not be reproduced, copied, edited, published, transmitted, or uploaded in any way without the written permission of Vibhor Asri and/or Vibhor Asri Publishing. Vibhor Asri Publishing does not grant any express or implied right to you under any of their trademarks, designs, service marks, course content, e-books, newsletters, audios, videos, blogs, copyrights, or other proprietary information.

No part of this Course may be reproduced or transmitted in any form or by any means, electronic or mechanical, without permission in writing from the Author.

Disclaimer: The advice and strategies found within may not be suitable for every situation. This work is sold with the understanding that neither the author nor the publisher is held responsible for the results accrued from the advice in this course.

Table of Contents

Introduction

There's an old saying in hunting: *You can ONLY eat what you kill.*

This applies to the profession of Selling also.

You can ONLY earn from what you sell.

This is the reason why Sales is such a challenging profession.

You can directly see the results of your performance.

In fact, Sales is the only department which brings money to the company. The rest of the departments are somehow involved in expenses.

Since salespeople are directly linked to their results, which can be easily measured, that's why they are the most accountable employees of the company.

On the one side, their job is highly vulnerable – anytime they can be fired.

But on the other side, the sky is the limit – if they are good at Selling.

That's why I love Selling so much, no matter in whatever way I sell.

But to become good at Selling, you need to learn how to close Sales.

In every sales process, there comes a time where the Sales need to be closed. Unfortunately, your customers won't always easily decide to buy.

At those times, you need arsenal of closing techniques so that you can make the sale. You need unusual creative ideas to assist you as per different circumstances when you're going to close the deal.

Selling is not an easy job.

Every day you must be looking for new prospects, identifying needs, making presentations, overcoming objections, and closing sales. It is really a hard job.

And out of all these activities, Closing is often the most painful part of the Sales process. It is the part that average salespeople dislike the most.

On the contrary, the top Salespeople are very good at Closing.

The fact that you live in a nice house with all the luxuries you own clearly tells us that someone sold that stuff to you. It was probably a good salesperson or a good sales copy in a magazine or online.

And it also tells us how to play this game with the sole objective to win - If someone is doing better than you, it is because they have learned the key skills before you have.

In this Course, I'm sharing many powerful closing techniques which you can use as per your wisdom.

I sincerely wish these methods could help you in closing more and more deals.

Good Luck!

Regards,

Vibhor Asri

Publisher & Editor,

Persuade and Grow Rich

Part One: Developing A Persistent Mindset of A Hardcore Closer

Defining Your Mission Statement

Selling is probably the oldest profession on this planet.

Every day we're selling ourselves, our products, our services to live the lifestyle we desire.

But it's not just a matter of more money or a better lifestyle for which we are in the business of selling.

The top salespeople have a mission in life that never stops them from moving forward… that never stops them from taking big risks… that never stops them from learning and becoming better and better.

I want you to define your own personal mission statement, no matter which company you work for.

This personal mission statement will give you the persistence to fight your daily battles without giving up.

Here are some questions which could help you in defining your personal mission statement…

- Why do customers remember me?

- How do customers feel after they deal with me?

- What do customers tell their friends about me?

- In what ways can I support others in my department?

- How does my department support the mission of my company?

You're Fired!

In my sales career, the worst thing I've experienced is seeing my colleagues getting fired from the job.

Whenever I see someone getting fired it disturbs me a lot.

I still remember some of the most upsetting incidents.

1st incident:

This was my first job. One of my colleagues was fired just in front of me.

We were having a routine weekly meeting with the Director where he fired my colleague because he had not closed even a single deal in his first 3 months.

My colleague was an extremely hard worker, meeting 3 to 5 new prospects almost every day.

Though he came from an MBA background, he was not a good communicator.

Moreover, he was not having a belief in himself that he could close the deal.

2nd incident:

In my next job, one of my colleagues was fired just after he returned from his honeymoon.

I remember him crying in front of me before leaving the office for the last time.

The reason was he closed just a few deals in his entire term in that company.

3rd incident:

One of my colleagues left the office the same day I came back from my vacation.

He was taking care of my work while I was on leave.

He didn't even tell me that the boss had fired him but asked him to take care of my work until I join back. You can imagine how emotional it was for me.

Again the reason was he closed very few deals.

4th incident:

One of my colleagues was fired while he was having lunch with his family. This time the reason was ego clash with the boss.

5th incident:

One of my colleagues was fired because he couldn't write a compelling promotional copy to bring hundreds of orders online.

He was a good content writer, a good researcher but missed the salesmanship skills in his writing.

I also remember the financial crisis of 2008-09, during which my department used to release a fresh list every month. This list was nothing but a warning to sales guys who topped the list:

"Be ready to get fired if you don't perform this month."

Fortunately, in my first few years of job, I always had a narrow escape from getting fired.

Of course, I have worked quite hard throughout my life. But it's not hard work that saved my sales career.

It's my willingness to learn, practice, and master selling skills that helped me to become better and better in this most lucrative profession in the world.

And that's what I demand from you.

Almost 1/3rd of salespeople drop out of the sales profession each year simply because they cannot deal with the customer's rejection and continuous pressure to bring sales.

This is because many people join the sales profession without any proper training.

Some people didn't get a job anywhere else. So they opt for sales to earn bread and butter.

Some people are not satisfied with their office job and think they can earn more by selling part-time.

Some people think they are born salespeople. They have a God gift to convince others.

Some people move accidentally into sales from other departments.

Some people are running their family business, that's why already involved in sales.

And some people want to become rich by starting and running their own business. And for this, they need to bring sales.

Since Sales doesn't require a 10th pass or 12th pass certificate, Degree, Diploma, Ph.D... unlike any other sophisticated profession... so one can start selling right from the first day without learning the science and art of Persuasion.

However, this is the biggest mistake done by every mediocre salesperson on the planet.

Selling is as serious as performing a critical surgery, arguing a case in court, or flying an airplane.

That's why many incompetent salespeople start quitting when they can't deal with challenges.

Their mind gets occupied in fears when they approach prospects, present their products & services, and most importantly when they try to close the deals.

This Course is designed for all those sales professionals who just want to not only survive in the sales profession but also want to thrive to make more and more money.

Why the Top 20% of Salespeople Make 80% of Money… And the Bottom 80% Make Only 20% of Money?

Some questions have kept me curious right from the beginning of my sales career.

Why some Salespeople are extremely successful, and others are just struggling to meet their ends?

What are these super salespeople doing differently from other ordinary salespeople?

Is it because of luck or hard work or attitude or some specialized knowledge that keeps them much ahead of the rest of mediocre salespeople?

During my research, I found there are many factors responsible for their tremendous success. But below traits are quite common among the top 20%...

Top salespeople are interested in multiplied salesmanship instead of selling one-to-one.

Top salespeople are interested in working on a BIG commission instead of working on a fixed salary.

Top salespeople believe in creative selling instead of conventional selling. They are always looking for more efficient ways to build the business.

And Top salespeople are continuously working on their salesmanship so that they can earn more and more in less time.

Now,

Multiplied salesmanship is not possible unless you are good at one-to-one selling.

The BIG commission is not achievable unless you are good at Closing.

Creative selling is not easy unless you are open to new ideas.

And continuously improving effectiveness is not promising unless you are targeting a definite aim.

Oh, I forgot to mention one more significant factor which immediately differentiates Winners from Losers.

The top 20% of salespeople are working towards achieving their WANTS, whereas the bottom 80% of salespeople are working enough just to satisfy their NEEDS.

So, it is very important to know what you WANT... why you WANT... when you WANT... and then how to achieve your WANT.

You Don't Need A Certificate or Even A World-Class Degree to Become A Good Salesperson

I've seen many people join sales because they don't have big impressive qualifications.

Of course, you don't need any world-class degree to become a good salesperson.

However, if you're selling any technical product or service, knowledge of that area is a must for you.

That's why many tech guys easily move into sales. Because they know the strengths and weaknesses of their product as well as of their competitor's products.

But this doesn't mean that these techies become good at selling. Knowledge of products is just the first step. To become supreme at selling, one needs to go through the college of hard knocks.

Salesmanship requires dealing with wins and losses.

Salesmanship requires dealing with rejections.

Salesmanship requires an understanding of human behaviour.

Salesmanship requires influencing your customer's mind.

Salesmanship requires mastering the process of persuasion.

You see, selling is as serious as any other profession.

It's a matter of your livelihood.

It's a matter of your prosperity.

It's a matter of providing the best to your family.

So, if you want to be a first-class at selling, be ready to go through the college of hard knocks.

Once you master this skill, you can't imagine how big the rewards can be.

Sometimes I receive inquiries from companies to know if I provide any certificate in my workshops.

I found it quite funny imagining I'm providing a certificate to a salesperson on which it's written: "This is to certify that _______ is trained by me personally, and now everyone should call him/her a Master Persuader."

Though it's quite amusing, I've seen such things.

For example:

Certificate in selling

Certificate in leadership

Certificate in writing

Certificate in computer programming

Certificate in reading, writing, speaking a foreign language

Certificate in music, singing, and dancing

Certificate in acting

Certificate in marketing (certificate in digital marketing is the latest trend)

Certificate in entrepreneurship

Moreover, these certificates are usually categorized as Beginner, Junior Practitioner, Practitioner, Master Practitioner, Advanced Practitioner, Trainer, Master Trainer, Advanced Trainer, Train the Trainer, etc. etc. etc.

My goodness, it sounds like a big franchise business.

It's so easy to get these certificates. What is needed from you is your hard-earned money and attendance.

Of course, there are some professions where degrees and certificates are a must to get before starting practice. For example, you can't ask a general physician to open your heart and do the surgery.

Likewise, you can't let a person fly an airplane without a pilot license.

But the skill-based professions don't need to distribute degrees and certificates to practitioners to confirm others they are eligible.

Here only one thing matters: **Performance**

If you keep performing, nobody will ever be bothered about who you are... from where you are... how much qualified you are... how much experienced you are...

No religion, caste, wealth, colour, language, age, gender, or place discrimination.

No such regrets as working under a more qualified but less experienced boss, just because you can't afford expensive degrees.

Sales is one such skill-based profession.

It is one of the most accountable professions, like sports, where everything is based on results.

But it's not only salespeople who need to be good at selling.

Business owners and self-employed should master salesmanship to bring new customers and repeat sales from existing customers.

And this becomes much more crucial in the digital age.

The Man Who Sold 13,001 Cars and Trucks

Let me tell you a true story.

The story of Joe Girard... the legendary Joe Girard... considered the greatest car salesman in the world... the man who sold 13001 cars and trucks in 15 consecutive years.

In 1963, Joe Girard joined the Chevrolet dealership as a Salesman. Before joining this car dealership, he had never sold any automobile in his entire life.

He knew nothing about cars and trucks. He joined the dealership because he had no other option when he left home to find any job so that he could buy food for his family.

Joe Girard borrowed $10 from his boss against the commission he owed on selling the first car. That $10 was the most precious thing for him because that money brought him groceries for his family.

From that day, he always remembered one simple arithmetic equation:

"Selling cars would bring him money, and that money would bring food to his family."

He became an aggressive salesman. He wanted to sell as many cars as possible.

He had tasted the success. He declared to himself that he would become the No.1 Salesman in town. He was exploring new strategies on how he could sell more cars every day.

But at the same time, he started facing opposition from his other colleagues not to be so aggressive.

So Joe Girard was facing competition not only from other brands, not only from other dealerships of Chevrolet but even from his own dealership staff.

But he wanted to sell more cars because he had seen the extreme pain of living without money.

So Joe Girard decided to become more enthusiastic and started exploring out-of-box thinking.

He became so creative in prospecting that every prospect wanted to deal with only and only Joe Girard.

And the rest is history.

The challenge is...

Can you become the next Joe Girard?

Then start applying out-of-box thinking in your job...

Why do People in Sales Quit?

Simply because they cannot deal with the rejection that is part and parcel of the business.

In the Classic book 'Think and Grow Rich', the author Napoleon Hill who had interviewed some of the richest and most successful people like Andrew Carnegie, John D. Rockefeller, Thomas Edison, Henry Ford, described six major fears that manage our life...

- **Fear of Poverty**

- **Fear of Criticism**

- **Fear of Ill-Health**

- **Fear of Old Age**

- **Fear of Death**

- **Fear of Loss of Love of Someone**

But I want to add two more fears to this list...

First is the **Fear of Rejection**.

And the other one is the **Fear of Failure**.

You see, these fears are not really bad.

They help us to take precautions. They help us to grow and prepare for the worst.

Fear of Ill-Health helps people to eat and live healthily.

Fear of Criticism helps people to behave well in society.

Fear of Failure helps people to work hard and smart.

Even industries exploit these fears to sell their products.

Fear of Criticism induces people to discard old clothes, old automobiles and replace them with new ones from time to time.

Fear of Rejection helps the cosmetic industry to sell expensive products to those who want to look attractive and win compliments from others.

But these fears also stop us from taking challenges because of which we go on to live a mediocre life.

For example, in the case of the Sales profession, Salespeople quit a lucrative sales career because of these reasons:

- Fear to make cold calls.

- Fear to approach strangers.

- Fear to give presentations in front of the audience.

- Fear to meet big shots.

- Fear to ask details from clients.

- Fear to answer objections.

- Fear to negotiate.

- Fear to ask closing questions.

- Fear to ask for promotion, commission, and bonus.

- And many, many more...

You see, these fears are **natural**.

We cannot ignore these fears. But these fears could affect our health if they occupy our minds all the time.

The question is how to combat them?

And the answer is we just need some knowledge. Fears will automatically vanish from our minds.

How I Saved My Sales Career with A Single Exercise?

Let me share one of my personal experiences because of which I was ready to quit Sales forever.

It happened at the beginning of my sales career. At that time, I was selling Engineering softwares to manufacturing companies and institutes.

It was a B2B Selling. First, I had to do cold calls, then to meet top executives and give presentations and demonstrations to their entire team. And finally, I had to close the deal and upsell other softwares.

One day I had an appointment with the Dean of one engineering college.

He was a retired military man. Since I waited outside his office for a long time, so he apologised for that and started telling me about his busy schedule.

And in return, I said, "I understand sir, you're a busy chap."

It was just a slip of the tongue that I called him "chap" due to my college time habits.

But it made him furious. He was extremely annoyed and told me to leave immediately otherwise he would complain to my boss.

I felt devastated. I never had such kind of experience before. I was shivering while returning home.

I decided that the sales profession was not for me.

Fortunately, at that time, I had already developed my habit of reading self-help books.

While going through some of the books, I found one good exercise on how to deal with a negative experience.

So, what I did exactly was I converted that scary experience into a funny scene.

How?

I imagined I'm sitting in a theatre, watching that particular scene when I was at the Dean's office.

Now to make it funny, I added some hilarious stuff to that scene.

I changed that office into a kind of small kids classroom.

I put some funny clothes on the Dean.

I changed his face into a clown, telling me how busy he was as he had to entertain everyone.

And the moment I spoke the word "chap", I changed his yelling into a silly song.

I made him stand up, start dancing and singing the song:

"You called me chap, chap, chap, chap, chap..."

"You called me chap, chap, chap, chap, chap..."

Also, I added some funny music in this scene.

It was not a one day exercise. It took me many days.

Gradually, the intensity of the painful experience was reduced.

And now I remember it as a funny incident.

The point is, **this exercise saved my sales career**.

If I had not performed the exercise on myself at that time, then I would have gone back to engineering and regretted my whole life for making a wrong decision.

Try this exercise if you had some very bad experiences recently, which is haunting you all the time.

While doing this exercise, don't try to be a perfectionist. Just be creative.

Remember, every situation is different. I never say to follow exactly what I'm saying. There are no rules in this game.

You need to apply your common sense as per the situation. You need to apply your creativity to see what suits you best.

The Story of A Super Successful Insurance Salesman

One of the common causes of failure is the habit of QUITTING when one is overtaken by temporary defeat.

In the classic book *Think and Grow Rich*, a holy book for millionaires, I read an inspirational story of Mr. R.U.Darby, who was considered one of the top insurance salesmen of his time.

Mr. Darby and his uncle, in search of a Gold mine, sold everything to purchase equipment and machines used for digging. But after months of digging, they lost hope and give up at one point, and sell all their equipment and machine to a local junkman.

The junkman, who was knowledgeable and wise, took advice from experts and started digging further in search of gold.

After digging just 3 feet from the point where Mr. Darby and his uncle stopped and left, the junkman found a huge mine of gold and became one of the richest people of that time.

This incident left a great impact on Mr. Darby, who then became one of the best insurance salesmen of all time because he said to himself that although he stopped from 3 feet gold, he would never stop when customers say NO to his proposal.

Whenever you face any tough situation, and a small monster thought comes to your mind of quitting, just recall this inspirational story and tell yourself, "Maybe I am just 3 feet from gold."

Don't Become A Desperate Salesperson

Tell me honestly did you want to become a salesperson since your childhood?

Did your parents want you to become a Salesperson one day?

I'm sure the answer is No. Am I right?

Have you ever thought why the Sales profession has earned such a bad reputation despite being one of the highest paying jobs in the world?

It's because people had bad experiences meeting desperate sales guys.

That's why many companies have a board outside their premises saying:

Salespeople Are NOT Allowed.

And many societies hire security guards just to stop them.

So, my friend, if you sell in desperation, I must tell you that you'll always have a tough time.

Desperation kills your negotiating power.

Desperation kills your self-respect.

Desperation kills your relationship with your customer.

To make it very simple:

No customer enjoys buying from desperate salespeople.

But they enjoy exploiting them.

So, start learning salesmanship if you never want to sell in desperation.

Is The Sales Career Right for You?

We feel very excited when we start something new in our lives, especially starting a new business or a job.

But sooner or later, when we don't achieve the desired success, we start raising doubts about ourselves and others.

We start blaming things that are not in our control, saying things like:

The economy is bad.

The recession is coming.

There are too many competitors.

People don't buy expensive things.

People don't try new things.

People are penny-savers.

Or we start giving excuses like:

I'm too old to do this.

I don't have the right qualification and experience.

I don't have a godfather in my industry.

I don't have contacts.

I don't have money to run a business.

And finally, one day, we quit and start exploring other options.

Wait!!!!

Can I say that since we know other options are available, that's why we quit?

So, basically, we quit because we were not getting success in our current venture, and we know that sooner or later, we will get a job somewhere else, or we can start some other business.

But what happens if you don't have boats to take you to some other place?

I mean, if you don't have any other options, then what will you do?

You will FIGHT.

You will fight with current circumstances.

You will fight with the corrupt system.

You will fight with your incompetence.

You will fight with everyone who suggests you quit and start something else.

So, burn your boats and keep fighting until you succeed.

Here are some basic traits that you need to develop when you chose a sales career for your livelihood:

- ✔ You have to be curious about everything in your business.

- ✔ You have to be extremely enthusiastic about your products and services.

- ✔ You should feel proud of yourselves that your products and services are going to change the life of millions of people.

- ✔ You should be perceived as extremely knowledgeable about your industry.

- ✔ You should be perceived as trustworthy.

- ✔ Even if you're not intelligent enough, you should be perceived as sincere in your efforts.

- ✔ You should be a problem solver. This is the only reason your customer wants to talk to you.

- ✔ If you want to become a leader in sales, then the conventional selling approach will not work. You have to think out-of-the-box. You have to become an Idea Man.

✔ You can't be rigid in the Sales profession. Be flexible in your strategies and approach.

✔ Instead of referring to yourself as a salesperson whose job is to sell products and services, you should consider yourself as an assistant buyer whose job is to assist your customers in getting the best deals that serve their interests. Can you see the difference between these two approaches?

✔ Adopt the *Better & Better* philosophy in whatever you do. Just like in the case of Martial Arts, in Selling, you need to learn a new technique and then practice it daily to become better at it. There is a Japanese management philosophy called *Kaizen*. It says small continuous improvements in all functions and by all people can improve the overall productivity. Adopt the same philosophy in your life to become better in your skills.

Before You Read Further

Before you read further, I want you to stop here and forget who you are, where you are, how bad or good your conditions are...

Instead, I want you to spend some time remembering your best memorable moments while answering these questions.

1) **What is your biggest sales achievement to date?**

    Achievement can be in terms of the monetary value of the deal, or recognition you got because of a single deal, or the most challenging deal of your life...

2) **What was your first sale as a professional?**

    It doesn't matter how small or big it was. What matters the most is the first time you tasted success in your professional life. And it becomes sweeter if it brought you some commission too.

3) **What was your first sale since your childhood?**

When you dig deep and try to remember the first sale in your life, you'll discover that you're selling somehow right from your childhood.

4) What was the most dramatic sales experience that you had in your life?

Here are some hints to understand what dramatic means:

- ✔ You were going to lose the deal, but at the last moment, you clinched the deal from your competitor.

- ✔ You were pitching your best selling item but sold the least popular or most expensive one. And for closing this deal, you got appreciation from everyone in your company.

- ✔ In the meeting with a potential client, you had an argument with a C-level executive, and you assumed you lost the sale. But the next day, you got the Purchase Order.

- ✔ The client called you and your competitor and asked both of you what you can provide the best deal. In the end, you grabbed the deal on a small point that hit your client's emotional triggers.

Sales is a lonely profession. Most of the time, you've to work alone. In this profession, nobody is going to motivate you daily. It's only YOU who can help yourself to remain self-motivated.

5 Basic Reasons: Why People NOT Buy from You?

There are five basic reasons people may not buy from you.

If you want to become successful in selling, never forget these reasons.

No Need

One of the reasons prospects may not buy from you is they do not feel they need what you are selling.

It's better not to waste time on these people unless you are confident that your product or service is definitely going to solve their problem.

Let me share one good example of how to sell these people…

In the 1980s and early 1990s, designers, architects, and draftsmen used to make drawings on paper and board since there was no CAD software in India.

So, when companies started selling CAD softwares to these designers, their initial response was, we don't need these softwares.

One of the reasons was these softwares were quite expensive.

Second, the designers were reluctant to work on computers.

So, how salespeople sold these expensive CAD softwares?

By simply showing them that the designers can delete, undo, copy, cut, paste, duplicate any part of the drawing whenever and wherever they want, which was impossible to do on paper.

In this way, marketers created the need for these softwares among designers.

So, unless you know the problem of your prospect in-depth, it's tough to sell to those who don't need your product.

Fortunately, we live in a world where people buy things not because they need them; people buy things because they **want** them.

If people start buying things only because they need them, imagine what would happen.

No bungalows, villas, penthouses would be required.

Why live in a villa when my small family can easily adjust to a one-bedroom apartment?

No expensive cars would be required.

Why buy expensive cars when we need them only for transportation?

No luxury watches would be required.

Why buy luxury watches when we need them just to see time?

No 5-star hotels and restaurants would be required.

Why go to an expensive restaurant when we need food just to satisfy our appetite?

No designer dresses would be required.

Why buy designer dresses from Malls when we can buy cheap clothes from our neighbourhood?

However, we can clearly see that every day people are buying big houses, expensive cars, luxury items, designer dresses, high tech gadgets, expensive food.

So, we're in the business of selling WANTS, not just Needs.

And the top salespeople are those who know **how to convert these Wants into Needs without which people cannot live.**

No Money

The second reason most people do not buy is they don't have any or enough money.

This is one of the most common excuses people give for not buying your products and services.

Examples:

I don't have money because the recession is coming, and I don't know what will happen next.

I don't have money because I lost my job.

I don't have money because I've started a new business.

I don't have money because I'm retired and living on a monthly pension.

I don't have money because I have the responsibility of my children's marriage.

I don't have money because I have to take care of my old parents.

I don't have money because I have a fixed monthly income, but my expenses are increasing.

Let me warn you: If you seriously want to build your career in sales, **don't buy your prospect's excuses.**

I have seen many salespeople qualify prospects based on how much money they can spend.

But I don't think this is the right way to qualify a prospect unless you're selling an extremely expensive product or service.

If someone is **seriously interested** in your product and believes he can't live without your product, one day, he would surely buy your product, no matter how poor he is. If it's required, he will borrow money from others to fulfill his desire or need.

No Desire

The third reason a lot of people don't buy from you is they do not really want what you are selling.

Remember, people buy things only when they want it more than their dear money to pay.

They are continuously comparing the value of your product with their hard-earned money they need to pay to get it.

That's why one of the most important tasks for us is to create the value of ourselves, our organization, and our products and services in the minds of people.

Have you seen the Weighing Scale?

On one side, you put cast-iron weights, and on the other side, you put the item you're buying.

Consider the prospect's mind as also a kind of Weighing Scale.

He is always comparing the **Value** of the product with the **Money** he is paying to get that product.

So, how can you create this Value in the prospect's mind?

By providing Emotional and Logical Reasons.

First, you need to look for the elements that create a sense of urgency to buy now.

Second, you need to gather the information that you could use to justify making a purchase now.

The more reasons you provide, the higher the value of your product and the heavier your side of the Weighing Scale.

And once you cross the equilibrium of the Weighing Scale in your favour… I mean, when the weight of the Value of your product becomes more than the weight of your prospect's money… the prospect will buy your product.

That's why people need sufficient emotional reasons that are compelling enough to give them a sense of urgency and sufficient logical reasons to justify buying now.

And the most important thing to keep in mind is that **people buy for their reasons, not yours.**

People don't care how many years, months, hours you have spent creating your product.

People don't care how much you love your product.

People don't care how desperate your situation is to sell your product to earn some money.

People don't care if you want to become a No.1 salesperson in your company.

People don't care if you want to spread your business worldwide.

People don't care if you want to take your family to Europe on vacation.

Therefore, if you want to close deals, make certain while trying to motivate your prospects, you discover their Emotional Reasons and Logical Reasons and don't sell them on your Emotional Reasons and Logical Reasons.

No Hurry

The fourth reason a lot of people don't buy is they're just not in a hurry.

It doesn't matter to them whether they buy today or tomorrow or next week or next month or even next year.

This is perhaps the toughest objection to deal with.

When you try to pitch them to buy your product, they will give an excuse that they have already spent half of their life without this product. So it doesn't make a big difference if they buy your product today or tomorrow.

That's why we need to create very attractive offers and provide a solid reason to buy NOW.

In this Course, you'll find a lot of ideas, techniques, and questions to close the deal fast.

No Trust

The fifth reason people don't buy from you is they don't trust you.

If you've spent years in selling, you know how critical this reason is.

Some people think you're lying.

You're suspicious.

You're misleading.

You're making too big claims.

You're desperate to get the order.

Rarely, these prospects will tell you on your face that you're a liar, but if they have the slightest of doubt on you, it will cost you a sale.

Also, people have some Fears that making a purchase could lead to pain.

For example:

1. Fear of making the wrong decision.

2. Fear of losing money.

3. Fear of criticism from family and friends, especially from the spouse.

4. Fear of getting scammed.

5. Fear of buying the wrong product.

6. Fear of buying a poor quality product.

7. Fear of buying more than actually required.

8. Fear of buying from strangers.

That's why you must follow a well-designed sales process to deal with the prospect's fears.

Types of Communication with Prospects

Nonflexible Communication

Nonflexible is a type of communication with the prospect where even if he loves the salesperson's product, then also he may never give the order.

This happens when both you and the prospect are rigid.

Means, both you and your prospect are fixed at their position.

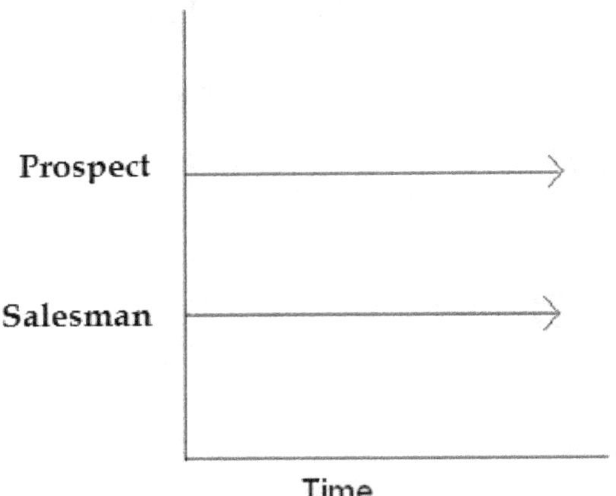

Both parties take fixed positions, and whenever they conduct meetings, it reinforces their original differences.

So, both of you don't want to discuss further.

Both of you don't want to negotiate.

The reasons could be many…

Not liking each other.

Ego clash or differences or misunderstanding.

Lack of interest from both sides in closing the deal.

This deal will never close unless one party takes the initiative. And generally, it's always a salesperson that needs to come up with some out-of-box thinking if he really wants to close the deal.

Polarized Communication

Polarized is a type of communication with the prospect, where the more the salesperson and the prospect talk to each other, the further they move away from closing the deal.

It happens when you and your prospect keep arguing with each other.

The more the two parties talk, the further apart they move.

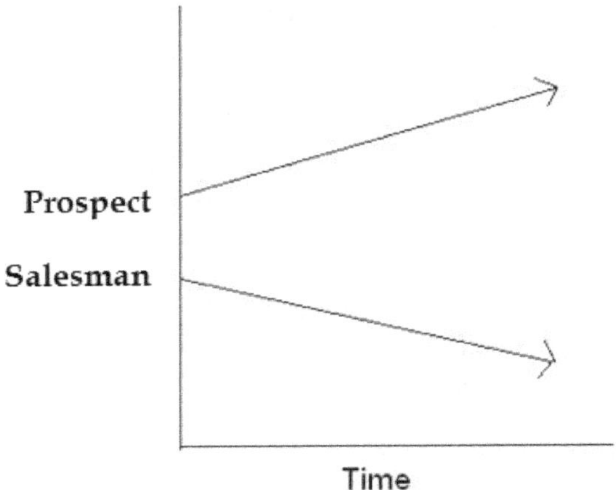

One party is moving to the North Pole while the other party is moving to the South Pole.

An argument is the worst form of communication if it has no reasoning.

However, the sales presentation is also an argument, but here you're presenting your case with facts and valid reasons, just like lawyers present the case in court.

The Negotiation

Negotiation is a type of communication with the prospect, which may bring sales most of the time but also keeps the salesperson struggling to get the most profitable deals.

It happens when both you and your prospect are flexible enough to discuss further.

Through Negotiation, both parties take steps to close the gap between them.

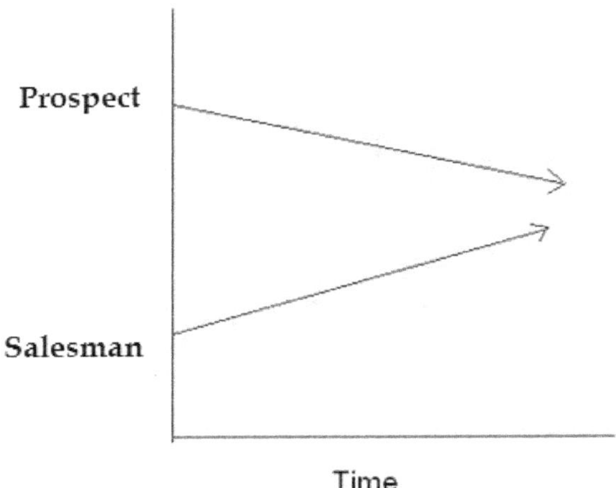

This is a positive sign that soon deals could be closed.

But it should be a Win/Win situation for both parties.

The Influence

Influence is a type of communication with the prospect where the prospect is buying on the salesperson's terms without raising any objections. It's a dream sale for every salesperson.

It happens when you master the principles and techniques of Influence and Persuasion.

Your prospect moves to the position held by you.

It's an ideal close for every salesperson because your prospect is buying on your terms and conditions.

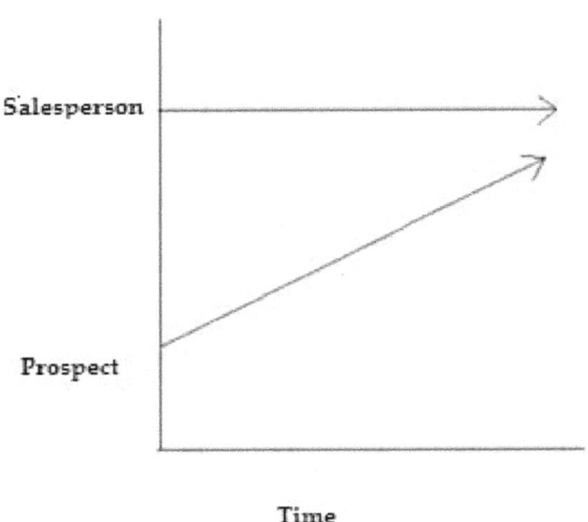

Here, the prospect finds so much value in you that he doesn't want to lose the deal.

This is the kind of communication you should aim for while closing every deal.

But remember, everything is good till it's ethical.

Conventional Sales Process

The entire Sales process can be divided into 10 Steps.

1. Prospecting: Hunting for new customers

2. Gathering information about your prospects

3. Start building rapport with your prospects

4. Identifying the wants and needs of your prospects

5. Qualifying your prospects

6. Presenting your solution

7. Overcoming objections of your prospects

8. Closing the deal

9. Bonding to build a long-term relationship with your customer

10. Getting referrals from your customers

However, to make the sales process simple to understand, I have categorized the entire process into three major categories...

1. Prospecting

2. Presenting

3. Closing

Top salespeople think about their income in terms of their **hourly rate** and want to make every hour productive.

Therefore, you need to remember that the only three activities that will pay your desired hourly rate are Prospecting, Presenting, and Closing.

Part Two: Mastering The Art of Selling

Prospecting: Hunting for New Customers

If you ask me which is the most critical part of the entire sales process, I would say it's Prospecting.

Sadly, many companies hire untrained newbies to do prospecting because senior people in the organization want to focus on closing big deals.

If you don't understand your market and your product, then you'll keep wasting your time, money, resources in meeting the wrong people.

But if you learn how to do prospecting, you will get good qualified leads right from the beginning, whether you're selling face-to-face or online. These are the people who will become your lifelong customers and ultimately help you in becoming rich.

The four important questions salespeople should remember while doing prospecting are:

1. Do you know the market for your Products?

2. How many prospects do you see every day?

3. At what part of the day do you see maximum prospects? Morning/Afternoon/Evening?

4. How much time do you spend talking to your prospects on the phone or meeting face-to-face?

Here's my Triangle Theory to highlight the importance of prospecting…

The Triangle Theory

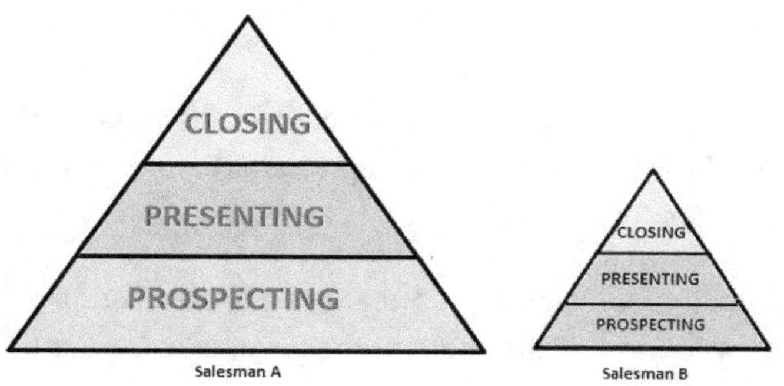

There are two triangles in the above picture. The big triangle represents Salesperson A, and the small triangle represents Salesperson B.

Both triangles are divided into three major activities of a salesperson.

1. Prospecting (the base area of a triangle)

2. Presenting (the middle area of a triangle)

3. Closing (the top area of a triangle)

It is clear from the picture that the entire business is dependent on Prospecting, which is the base area of the triangle.

The total area of Prospecting represents the total number of cold calls or cold meetings the salesperson has done in an entire month.

The total area of Presenting represents the total number of prospects who have seen the entire presentation/demonstration of a salesperson in a month.

The total area of Closing represents the total number of prospects who have finally bought the product in a month.

What do you think out of these two, who is more successful?

Salesperson A or Salesperson B?

Obviously, it's clear from the picture that Salesperson A is more successful, simply because he has closed more deals.

But what's the reason he has closed more deals?

The reason lies in the base of the triangle, which represents the prospecting part of the Sales process.

The larger the base of the triangle, the larger the upper section, which represents the Closing part of the Sales process.

So, in layman's terms, how many deals you have closed is **directly proportional** to how many sales call you have made at the time of prospecting.

Top salespeople are always doing prospecting wherever they go, even on holidays.

But it doesn't mean you blindly do prospecting. You need to choose your prospects carefully.

You need to qualify them.

How?

By knowing your prospective customers as much as possible.

It's critical to have information about your customers.

Armed with the right knowledge, you can outsell your competition.

Knowing your customer means knowing what your customer really wants.

Look, listen, and learn all you can about the customer, both personally and professionally. You'll find topics for opening conversations, which can open doors for you and your company.

Presenting Your Solution

Presenting covers your entire sales pitch.

Every part of the presentation should be planned carefully. You should know…

What to say? How to say? When to say?

How to answer the prospect's objections?

When to move towards Closing?

The better the rapport you have with your prospect, the better the chances he will listen to your entire sales pitch.

The rapport creation process should start immediately when meeting the other person.

While building rapport, observe the conscious and unconscious responses of your prospect.

If the prospect shows any resistance, then immediately change your rapport technique.

Features and Benefits

Features are cold, remote, and impersonal; benefits are warm and tempting.

While prospects can be interested in features, it is BENEFITS that cement the sale.

Each time you describe a benefit in a sales presentation, purchasing desire increases.

For example:

Computer Features and Their Benefits

Features	Benefits
Intel Core i5 processor	Lets you both work faster and use the latest video and graphics applications.
4 GB Memory and 1 TB HDD	Holds more programs and data files giving you more power and flexibility.
19.5-inch screen	Gives you an increased viewing area without taking any more disk space than a 17-inch screen.

How to Sell Like Steve Jobs

In the last two decades, Apple has gained huge popularity and market share in several countries.

In fact, in 2018, Apple became the world's first company to reach a trillion-dollar market cap.

All over the world, people are crazy about Apple's products, no matter how expensive they are. They get excited whenever Apple launches a new product.

It was Steve Jobs, the co-founder of Apple, who launched many of Apple products himself. For example, iPod, iPhone, iPad.

We all remember Steve Jobs as a great entrepreneur... a great business leader... a great tech visionary.

His contribution in transforming a small startup into one of the world's top companies was simply outstanding.

However, Steve Jobs was also a great salesman. His product launching presentations are considered some of the best sales pitches of all time.

It was Steve Jobs's passion, enthusiasm, and love for his revolutionary products that made him a super presenter.

Here are some of his presentation quotes which clearly show how enthusiastic Steve Jobs was about his products:

"Introducing three revolutionary products"

"World's thinnest notebook"

"1,000 sounds in your pocket"

"Reinvent the phone"

"Think different"

"Macintosh changed the whole computer industry"

"iPod changed the entire music industry"

Two lessons that we can learn about salesmanship from Steve Jobs's presentations:

First, always sell a product you are excited about.

Second, even if you're selling great ideas, products, concepts... the difference lies in the presentation.

An idea is powerless if you don't know how to present it.

So, if you want to sell your ideas to customers, investors, management, employees, family, and friends, you need to master your presentation skills.

42 Most Seductive Words in The World of Selling

1. Name

2. Please

3. Benefit

4. Security

5. Thank You

6. Trust

7. Because

8. Value

9. Exciting

10. Deserve

11. How to

12. Fun

13. Honest

14. Free

15. Love

16. Right

17. Powerful

18. Results

19. Discovery

20. You / Your

21. Quality

22. Joy

23. Money

24. Beautiful

25. Vital

26. Proud

27. Easy

28. Proven

29. Health

30. Profit

31. New

32. Truth

33. Expert

34. Save

35. Comfort

36. Advantage

37. Improved

38. Investment

39. Guarantee

40. Happy

41. Safety

42. Now

How to Use These Seductive Words in Your Sales Pitch

Start using these words in your daily conversation with your prospects, in your emails, in your brochures, websites, advertisements, and other promotional materials.

Here are some examples of how to use these words in your daily sales pitch:

- "This is a very **powerful** car. You will feel **proud** and **happy** to be the owner of this car."

- "Our brand and our dealership completely focus on **Quality**. We **guarantee** customer satisfaction."

- "This product/service is **guaranteed,** so **you** can feel **secure** in making a decision now."

- "**You** will **love** this DVD Player. Along with it, we are giving three DVDs absolutely **free** of your choice."

- "Consider this **beautiful** house as an **investment** and **security, because** here you're going to spend the rest of your life with your family, whom **you love** the most."

- "Mr. Prospect, let me warn you… since **you're** making such a **vital** decision, **you** should deal with only **proven experts** like me instead of dealing with a newbie."

- "That's **beautiful**, isn't it?"

Imagine you run an online business selling designer dresses. The success of your advertising campaign will depend on the way you phrase your offer. You have come up with 3 ways to present the same offer:

a) Half price

b) Buy one – get one **free**

c) 50% off

Which one is most effective?

The answer is **b**. Because it contains the most seductive word in the world - FREE.

What Words to Use While Speaking or Writing to Visual Prospects

Visual people represent things in their minds with Pictures.

- ❖ Look

- ❖ See

- ❖ Appear

- ❖ Focus

- ❖ Clarity

- ❖ Glance

- ❖ Notice

- ❖ Perceive

- ❖ Sight

- ❖ Observe

- ❖ Picture

- ❖ Show

- ❖ View

- ❖ Light

- ❖ Obvious

- ❖ Watch

- ❖ Preview

- ❖ Survey

- ❖ Imagine

- ❖ Picture

- ❖ Perspective

- ❖ Bright

- ❖ Diagrams

- ❖ Envision

- ❖ Illustrate

- ❖ Highlight

- ❖ Videos

- ❖ Charts

- ❖ Reflect

Selling to Visual Prospects

- "Can't you just **picture** your family having dinner together in this lovely dining room?"

- "Do you **see** what I mean?"

- "**Imagine** how all the walls will **look** when we put these **pictures**."

- **Notice** how **bright** your room **looks** now with this window."

- "Did you **observe** how that worked?"

- "**Look** inside this car. Aren't these seat covers **gorgeous**?"

- "I'm sure you can **see** how that would work for you, right?

What Words to Use While Speaking or Writing to Auditory Prospects

Auditory people represent things in their mind with sound and words.

- ❖ Gossip

- ❖ Audio

- ❖ Speech

- ❖ Articulate

- ❖ Interview

- ❖ Loud

- ❖ Pitch

- ❖ Voice

- ❖ Noise

- ❖ Say

- ❖ Express

- ❖ Resonate

- ❖ Talk

- ❖ Click

- ❖ Hear

- ❖ Accent

- ❖ Ask

- ❖ Listen

- ❖ Remark

- ❖ Sound

- ❖ Tone

- ❖ Sounds good

- ❖ Discuss

- ❖ Inquire

- ❖ In tune

- ❖ Static

- ❖ Speak

- ❖ Tell

- ❖ Ring

❖ Mention

Selling to Auditory Prospects

Let auditory prospects know that you are speaking in their language. Hearing these words will make them relax and open to you.

When you sell to auditory prospects, tell them about all the auditory features your product has.

Here are some examples of how to use auditory words in your daily language:

- "How does this **sound** so far?"

- "Does this **ring a bell** with you?"

- "That's what you want to **hear**, isn't it?"

- "How does that price **sound**?"

- "Can you **tell** why this is more efficient?"

- **"Sound** reasonable?"

- "I want you to **hear** yourself **how smoothly the engine runs**."

- "Is this **sounding** like it might work for you?"

- "Let's **discuss** how we can solve your problem through our services."

- "I'm sure once I **tell** you my offer, it'll **sound like music to your ears**."

- "If you die without enough insurance, you are going to leave your family financially **dejected and rejected**."

What Words to Use While Speaking or Writing to Kinesthetic Prospects

Kinesthetic people represent things in their minds with feelings and sensations.

- ❖ Emotional
- ❖ Relax
- ❖ Hassle
- ❖ Pressure
- ❖ Hold
- ❖ Touch
- ❖ Tension
- ❖ Charge
- ❖ Foundation
- ❖ Shift
- ❖ Feel

- ❖ Comfortable

- ❖ Handle

- ❖ Grab

- ❖ Contact

- ❖ Rub

- ❖ Suffer

- ❖ Hit

- ❖ Affect

- ❖ Impress

- ❖ Tackle

- ❖ Know

- ❖ Understand

- ❖ Worry

- ❖ Breathe

- ❖ Massage

Selling to Kinesthetic Prospects

Give them things to touch. If you do so, you'll be able to sell them 3 times faster.

Instead of just showing a brochure to your clients, make sure they can hold it. Although they may look at the pictures or listen to your details, what matters the most to them is that they have these materials in hand.

Examples:

- "Just **hold** the mouse and **know** how it **feels** while moving."

- "May I ask you to **sit on this Sofa in a relaxed position, feel its texture**? You'll **know** yourself how **comfortable** it is while watching TV… talking with friends… reading books."

- If you're selling cars, think of all the different surfaces you can let them touch: "Mr. Prospect, let's go for a test drive with your family. Check yourself whether seats are **comfortable** or not while driving. **Move** the gear shift to check whether it's **smooth** or **hard**. **Adjust the**

dashboard controls as per your requirements. Try to **press the body with both hands** to check how **strong** it is. Also, **kick the tires with your full force**."

- "How do you **feel** about it?"

- "I hope you **understand** how important this insurance for your family is. They will never **worry** about finance if in case something happens to you."

Hypnotic Words

These words subtly affect the prospects' minds without their notice.

Since most of our decisions are made by our subconscious mind, whether it's a simple task or a crucial project, therefore, these words could directly hit on the prospect's subconscious mind to take immediate action.

"-ly" Hypnotic Words

- Obviously

- Apparently

- Certainly

- Clearly

- Gently

- Softly

- Luckily

- Fortunately

- Happily

Comparative Hypnotic Words

- Faster

- Slower

- Fancier

- Lighter

- Stronger

- More

- Better

- Nicer

- Quicker

- Easier

Example (Recruitment Speech):

"This Company is getting bigger and bigger and better and better. Why don't you join NOW?"

Absolutes Hypnotic Words to Build Conviction

❖ Always

❖ Never

❖ Nothing

Examples:

- "You have made an excellent selection. People are **always** happy with that model."

- "That's a fine choice. You will **never** regret making this decision."

- "There is **nothing** out there that can perform like this system."

"-est" Superlatives Hypnotic Words

❖ Fastest

❖ Strongest

❖ Easiest

❖ Simplest

❖ Deepest

❖ Best

❖ Greatest

❖ Toughest

Unusual / Seductive / Control Offers

Unusual offers are those which could be highly risky and not easy to adopt in a business unless you are ready to face criticism or losses. These could be bold offers. These could be very creative offers. These offers could put a challenge to customers to check themselves if you deliver to your promise or not.

Seductive offers are those which immediately take your prospects' attention, make them forget about your competitors, break their loyalty with existing vendors, and force them to take immediate action to grab your offer.

Control offers are those that are running for a long time, precisely for more than 3 years continuously. Although during this period, marketers keep testing different offers to check which offer brings the best results, the Control offer always wins.

Here are a few examples of Unusual/Seductive/Control offers that grabbed my attention.

Example #1

This offer was targeted at wealthy individuals who could be persuaded to buy a diesel car.

It was one of the most unusual offers ever made by a car company. They came out with such an offer just to show the benefits of buying a diesel car.

As a result, the sales letter was responsible for selling one of the first diesel cars of Mercedes in the USA. At that time, Mercedes decided to junk the production of diesel cars because of some disadvantages associated with it. Like:

- At that time, Diesel fuel was not available everywhere.

- Gasoline was relatively cheap in those days.

- Diesel engines were very noisy as compared to standard gasoline engines.

....

You -- and a small number of others -- have been selected to receive the most unusual offer ever made by a car manufacturer.

I will pay for all fuel, all motor oil, all oil filters, and all lubrications on the new Mercedes-Benz 190 Diesel for the first 15,000 miles you drive it.

This offer is from Mercedes-Benz of North America. It is not from your Mercedes-Benz dealer. It will not affect your trade-in or terms in any way. I feel certain you will like this car and will help me spread the word about it.

That's why I can offer you all fuel free. All motor oil free. All oil filters free. All lubrications free. All are yours free for the first 15,000 miles you own and drive your new Mercedes-Benz 190 Diesel.

No other manufacturer of a full-size 4-door sedan in the entire world could afford to make this offer.

I can make it because the Mercedes-Benz 190 Diesel averages over 30 miles per gallon of diesel fuel -- and diesel fuel costs 1/3 less than gasoline in many states.

In fact, the 190 Diesel regularly saves its owners more than 50 percent on fuel costs alone.

And, like all Mercedes-Benz cars, the 190 Diesel is so finely machined it uses scarcely any motor oil.

That's not all.

The 190 Diesel never needs a tune-up. It has no carburetor to adjust or replace. No spark plugs, no points, no condensers, no distributor.

....

Example #2

At the time when Joe Karbo wrote this direct response advertisement to sell his book *The Lazy Man's Way to Riches*, it was not common to use such bold offers of not cashing the cheque for a specific period. But Joe Karbo's sales letter proved that persuasive copy + superb offer is not 1+1=2. It becomes 1+1=11.

Joe sold over 3 million copies of his self-published book without ever being available in a bookstore.

A big credit goes to the offer, which was bold and unusual at that time.

....

What if I'm so sure that you will make money my Lazy Man's Way that I'll make you the world's most unusual guarantee?

And here it is: I won't even cash your check or money order for 31 days after I've sent you my material.

That will give you plenty of time to get it, look it over, try it out.

If you don't agree that it's worth at least a hundred times what
you invested, send it back. Your uncashed check or money
order will be put in the return mail.

The only reason I won't send it to you and bill you or send it
C.O.D. is because both these methods involve more time and
money.

....

Example #3

I always say business, and especially marketing and advertising is all about coming up with unique big ideas that nobody has thought of before.

But these ideas come only when you understand your market so well that you know what your market is missing in their life... what they are craving for... what they are not going to live without it...

And then you come up with a simple but brilliant idea which brings hope and enthusiasm in their lives... which satisfy their lifelong curiosity and desire... and which provides the solution to the desperation that your market knew somewhere inside but never able to acknowledge it, and moreover never able to express it to others.

But it was you who studied your market so well that you know their deepest pains and desires, which they have never shared with others consciously.

Here is an example of one such idea. It's a letter written by a great marketer, entrepreneur, and copywriter, Gary Halbert, who was struggling financially at that time. So, it's become a do or die for him to come up with some unique idea on which he could make a large amount of money.

And what he did is a perfect example of how a big idea emerges by studying your market.

Gary found one of the common interests amongst people is to know about their family history. So, he came up with a solution to satisfy this lifelong curiosity. And for this, he categorized people according to their last name and sent a common letter addressing a particular last name. For example, Dear Mr. Macdonald in the below letter.

Do you want to know how successful this letter was? This 1-page letter, considered as one of the most mailed sales letters ever written, was mailed for more than 30 years to more than 600 million people.

At its height, this sales letter was making more than $200,000 a day.

This letter brought in around 20,000 orders per day and more than 7 million orders in total. Processing these orders became such a big task that the bank created a separate section, and Gary Halbert hired 30 full-time employees just to make bank deposits.

Later, the company sold for $75 million.

This letter is an example of how great marketers think and work. When you read this letter, you will find that the idea behind this letter has nothing to do with your company, industry, expertise, experience, degrees & diplomas, and even your brand, on which companies spend millions and billions.

Since it's a short letter, I'm sharing the entire letter with you and not just the offer part.

....

Dear Mr. Macdonald,

Did you know that your family name was recorded with a coat-of-arms in ancient heraldic archives more than seven centuries ago?

My husband and I discovered this while doing some research for some friends of ours who have the same last name as you do. We've had an artist recreate the coat-of-arms exactly as described in the ancient records. This drawing, along with other information about the name, has been printed up into an attractive one-page report.

The bottom half of the report tells the story of the very old and distinguished family name of Macdonald. It tells what the name means, its origin, the original family motto, its place in history and about famous people who share it. The top half has a large, beautiful reproduction of an artist's drawing of the earliest known coat-of-arms for the name of Macdonald. This entire report is documented, authentic and printed on parchment-like paper suitable for framing.

The report so delighted our friends that we have had a few extra copies made in order to share this information with other people of the same name.

Framed, these reports make distinctive wall decoration and they are great gifts for relatives. It should be remembered that we have not traced anyone's individual family tree but have researched back through several centuries to find out about the <u>earliest</u> people named Macdonald.

All we are asking for them is enough to cover the added expenses of having the extra copies printed and mailed. (See below.) If you are interested, please let us know right away as our supply is pretty slim. Just verify that we have your correct name and address and send the correct amount in cash or check for the number of reports you want. We'll send them promptly by return mail.

Sincerely,

Nancy L. Harbert

P.S. If you are ordering only one report, send two dollars ($2.00). Additional reports ordered at the same time and sent to the same address are one dollar each. Please make checks payable to me, Nancy L. Halbert.

....

Example #4

If you're selling high-paid consultancy services, then you need to look at this unusual offer. Since your time is very precious, your marketing and advertising should incorporate a **qualifying process** so that you don't waste your time dealing with the wrong clients.

I took this offer from the advertisement 'The Amazing Secret Of A Marketing Genius Who Is Afraid To Fly' promoting Jay Abraham's services. Abraham is considered a marketing wizard and one of the best strategic thinkers in the world.

This letter is unusual because every prospective client has to fulfil at least 6 conditions before taking Jay Abraham's services.

....

Can this man help you? Can he, for example, double your gross sales in less than 90 days as he has done for so many others? Can he, as he has done in some cases, triple your cash flow in less than 36 hours?

Maybe. Maybe not. You can find out with one telephone call. But before you waste your time and dime you should give some thought to the six principal reasons he may not be able to help you. You see, Mr. Abraham freely admits he cannot help everyone or every business (and there are many he wouldn't help if he could). Here then are the six minimum conditions that must exist in order for it to make sense for you to contact Mr. Abraham.

1. You must have enough money to finance a serious first-class sales effort.

2. You must have an ethical first class product or service. (Even the best marketing strategies will fail if your customers perceive you have an inferior product)

3. You must be able to handle an almost overnight increase in sales. Here is why. Mr. Abraham is very expensive. However, the bulk of his income comes in the form of commissions from your increased cash flow which will be generated by his expertise. Therefore, if you can't handle more business now, don't call him until you can.

4. You must have an open mind. Mr. Abraham's methods are unique to say the least. As he puts it, "I won't travel or spend time massaging anyone's ego. Therefore, when it comes to money, I am forced to go right for the jugular."

5. Your operation must already be somewhat profitable. Mr. Abraham can help almost anyone with potential but even he cannot multiply zeroes!

6. And finally, needless to say, if you crave Mr. Abraham personal contact, you must go to him. Otherwise, you must be content to work via mail, telephone, telex, telegram, telecopier, or carrier pigeon.

By the way, there is just one more thing. Please don't call unless you yourself own or control the business. If you can't make the ultimate decisions, just give the phone to whoever can Please.

....

Example #5

At the beginning of this issue, I talked about *The Wall Street Journal* sales letter, which generated more than 1 billion dollars in sales.

It was just a 2-page letter which ran for around 25 years with almost the same offer. Price changed from time to time.

Here's the offer part of that sales letter. Though it's a simple subscription offer, we can't afford to ignore it if it brought so much money.

Remember, there is only one criterion to measure the success of any marketing campaign: SALES. Everything else is just a show-off in the world of fake PR news. Unfortunately, people easily get influenced by PR stories if they don't dig deep.

....

A Money-Saving Subscription

Put our statements to proof by subscribing for the next 13 weeks for just $44. This is among the shortest subscription terms we offer – and a perfect way to get acquainted with The Journal.

Or you may prefer to take advantage of our better buy – one year for $149. You save over $40 off the cover price of The Journal.

Simply fill out the endorsed order card and mail it in the postage-paid envelope provided. And here's The Journal guarantee: Should The Journal not measure up to your expectations, you may cancel this arrangement at any point and receive a refund for the undelivered portion of your subscription.

If you feel as we do that this is a fair and reasonable proposition, then you will want to find out without delay if The Wall Street Journal can do for you what it is doing for millions of readers. So please mail the enclosed order card now, and we will start serving you immediately.

....

And assurance in the end.

....

An Investment In Success

I cannot promise you that success will be instantly yours if you start reading The Wall Street Journal. But I can guarantee that you will find The Journal always interesting, always reliable, and always useful.

....

Example #6

The story of Domino's Pizza is inspirational for young entrepreneurs.

In the early 1960s, when two brothers, Tom and James Monaghan, bought a small restaurant, they never thought that one day it would become a billion dollars business.

In fact, within a few months, James left the business to continue his full-time job as a postman. I'm sure he would have regretted his decision his whole life. What an opportunity he missed to make millions instead of peanuts.

On the other side, the restaurant business started growing rapidly. Within a few years, Tom Monaghan purchased two more restaurants in the same county.

But Tom didn't stop there. He started franchising business all over the nation and then to other countries.

In the next four decades, Domino's Pizza became a global brand.

Just like any other successful business, there were many factors responsible for the growth of Domino's Pizza, like innovation, quality, a perfect business model, incorporating the latest technologies, sound operations, great service, and brilliant advertising.

But it was an unusual offer which not just became their USP, in fact, crushed competition locally, then nationally, and later internationally.

Yes, you guessed it right.

I'm talking about their famous 30 MINUTES OR FREE PIZZA Delivery guarantee.

This is one of the most famous and boldest offers in the restaurant business.

Ironically, this unusual offer came out as a solution to the problem of having limited seats in a small restaurant building because of which they couldn't accommodate more customers.

Moreover, they studied human behaviour. When we are hungry, we want food fast. When we see an offer like 30 minutes or free pizza, we get assurance that we've to wait for a maximum of 30 minutes to satisfy our hunger. Imagine if it was 60 minutes instead of 30, then was it possible for Domino's to get the same level of success?

This unusual offer was a blessing in disguise, which turned a local small-sized restaurant into a billion dollars global business.

Although, after some legal issues, this offer was withdrawn, still, it's running in a few countries with some terms & conditions.

Example #7

This is one of the best examples of selling a high-ticket item to the affluent.

The letter was sent to owners of large boats and jets and talked about a 26-day expedition throughout the world's polar regions in detail.

The biggest point about this letter is that **it made the reader feel like a country hero** by accepting the invitation and going on this mission.

The letter starts with a great offer.

....

Dear Mr. ______,

As Chairman of the Admiral Richard E. Byrd Polar Center, it is my privilege to invite you to become a member of an expedition which is destined to make both news and history.

It will cost you $10,000 and about 26 days of your time. Frankly, you will endure some discomfort, and may even face some danger.

On the other hand, you will have the rare privilege of taking part in a mission of great significance for the United States and the entire world. A mission, incidentally, which has never before been attempted by man.

You will personally harp the chance to help enrich mankind's fund of knowledge about two of the last earthly frontiers, the polar regions.

I am inviting you to join a distinguished group of 50 people who will fly around the world longitudinally, over both poles, on an expedition which will commemorate Admiral Richard E. Byrd's first Antarctic flight in 1929.

Among the highlights of this transpolar flight – the first commercial flight ever to cross both poles and touch down on all continents – will be stopovers at the American military/scientific bases at Thule, Greenland, and McMurdo Sound, Antarctica.

Because this expedition has the interest and support of much of the Free World, you and your fellow members will be honored guests (in many cases, even celebrities) at state and diplomatic receptions throughout the itinerary. You will have the opportunity to meet and talk with some of the world's important national leaders and public figures, such as Pope Paul VI, the Emperor of Japan, General Carlos Romulo, and many others who are already a part of history.

By agreeing to join this expedition, you will, in a sense, establish yourself in history too. For you will become a

Founding Trustee of the new Admiral Richard E. Byrd Polar Center, sponsor of the expedition.

Your biography will be recorded in the Center's archives, available to future historians. The log, photographs and memorabilia of the expedition will be permanently displayed in the Center. And your name will be inscribed, with those of the other expedition members, on a bronze memorial tablet.

....

Again, the letter ends with more details on the offer.

....

As mementos of the expedition, you will receive a leather-bound, personalized copy of the logbook and a piece of the fabric from Admiral Byrd's original plane, mounted in crystal.

You will also be presented with a framed certificate from the Admiral Richard E. Byrd Polar Center, affirming your appointment as a Founding Trustee and expressing appreciation for your interest in, contributions to and efforts on behalf of the Center and its objectives. In the future, you will be kept fully advised of the plans and activities of the Center, and be invited to participate to whatever extent you wish. And of course, you will have lifelong access to the Center's archives and services.

Most important, you will take back with you a once-in-a-lifetime experience. The day may come when journeys to and over the poles are commonplace. But today, the privilege is available to very few.

It is true, I think that this privilege does carry responsibility with it. By the time you return, you will have received a comprehensive indoctrination course in the polar regions by the world's leading authorities. Your responsibility will be to make the most of the knowledge you will gain, to become an active advocate – perhaps even a disciple – of polar research and development.

It is a responsibility which, I trust, will weigh easily upon you. For once the polar air has been absorbed into your bloodstream, there is no cure. Like others who have been stricken, you will probably find yourself reading every word you can find on the North and South Poles. And most likely, thinking about your next trip.

But first of all, you must decide about this trip. If you have a sense of adventure, a certain pioneering spirit, and if the prospect of taking part in a mission of worldwide significance and historical importance appeals to you, perhaps you should consider joining the expedition. It is doubtful that you will have ever have another chance like this.

Obviously, you can't make a decision of this magnitude instantly. But a word of caution: reservations will be accepted in the order received – a total of only 60, including ten standbys. The departure date, remember, is November 8, 1968, so there is little time to waste.

The price of $10,000 includes food and beverages, all accommodations (the best available under all circumstances) transportation, special clothing, insurance, side excursions – virtually everything except your travel to and from Boston.

Money received will go into escrow at the United States Trust Company in Boston until the time of the flight. To the extent that revenues from the trip will exceed costs, the activities of the Polar Center will be accelerated.

To reserve your place in the expedition, just drop me a note on your letterhead or personal stationery, with your deposit check for $2,500, made out to the United States Trust Company. Incidentally, if anything prevents your leaving as planned, you can send another in your place; otherwise, cancellations cannot be accepted later than 30 days before departure.

....

Example #8

I conduct public workshops called *Persuasion Mastery Workshop* in different cities from time to time. In these workshops, I teach the principles and techniques of Persuasion.

This is my control offer, which I ran for many years and got very good results.

....

Special Corporate Offers

1 Enrolment @ ______

2 Enrolment : 10% Off on Regular Price @ ______

3 Enrolment : 15% Off on Regular Price @ ______

4 Enrolment : 20% Off on Regular Price @ ______

5 Enrolment : 25% Off on Regular Price @ ______

<u>ENROLL NOW</u>

The Enrolment Fee includes Lunch, Tea, and Study Material. The workshop is non-residential.

Limited Seats Only. **15** Participants (max) to be enrolled for making it an interactive brainstorming session. Enrolment will be done on a First Come First Serve basis.

....

Example #9

I love this example because it shows how a small family business, finding premium-quality nuts from all over the world and selling to their customers in the entire country, has built a multi-million dollar business by adopting the direct response advertising (also known as mail-order) model.

What I like in their sales letter is **the process they follow** to give their customers the best quality nuts.

Here it is:

....

- Our buyers travel the world over searching for the biggest, best, most perfect nuts we can find.

- We contract for the best in advance – before they are even ready for harvest – and before our competitors can snap them up.

- We select them, grade them, shell them, pick them over by hand, roast them carefully, and choose only the biggest, best, "Premium Grade" hand-selected nut meats for our mail order business.

- (Because the supply of this top grade of nuts is so limited, we don't have enough to sell them through retail stores. So we save all the very best nuts to sell you direct-by-mail.)

- We package them for delivery to you in our unique "Shell Pack," which sucks out all the air and keeps the nuts as safe and fresh as when they leave our plant.

- We sell them to people like you – by mail – at prices well below what you'd expect to pay for this premium grade. We offer very fancy nuts at very "un-fancy" prices.

- We give you all the value we can, and it's always more than you pay for, in the hopes you'll buy from us again and again.

....

But I have not included this example because of their process. This newsletter issue is all about exceptional offers, like the **three guarantees** mentioned in the sales letter.

See yourself:

....

And to ensure that we live up to all this (and to our family tradition), we put ourselves on the spot with this triple guarantee:

<u>FRESHNESS GUARANTEE</u>: We guarantee our nuts to be the freshest you can buy. Our exclusive vacuum "shell pack" keeps them as fresh as if they were in their own shells.

<u>SAFE DELIVERY GUARANTEE</u>: We guarantee safe delivery to you. You don't have to worry about squashed packages or broken nuts. Again, the unique "Shell Pack" protects your nuts.

<u>TOTAL SATISFACTION GUARANTEE</u>: We guarantee your satisfaction when you buy our nuts – no matter what. If for any reason you should ever be displeased, simply return the unused nuts to us for replacement or an immediate full cash refund.

....

And at the end of the letter, you will find another guarantee:

....

And to make our offer even more appealing, I'll throw in a free gift when you try our nuts. Send in your order and I'll send you a free Taster Box of our giant "two-bite cashews." It's another small way for us to give you a little more than you pay for.

So please order now and see for yourself. You won't be disappointed. (That's our fourth guarantee.)

....

Example #10

When you're absolutely confident about your services, then you should **challenge your market to try you without any risk**.

This is what a startup advertising agency *Callas, Powell, Rosenthal & Bloch* did in their most famous advertisement for promoting their own services. In fact, this advertisement was responsible for establishing the advertising agency and bringing so many qualified leads that they had never looked for work desperately.

Gary Bencivenga, one of the best copywriters in the world, wrote the ad.

Here's how this ad begins with its bold challenge. And yes, there are some conditions too.

....

If you are a direct response advertiser, here is a no-risk offer from Callas, Powell, Rosenthal & Bloch...

We'll guarantee to outpull your best ad by at least 10% in a split-run test.

If we don't pull at least 10% more responses, you won't owe us
a penny for any work we've done – creative or production.
We'll even refund half your media expense, to cover our half
of the test.

If we do beat your best ad by at least 10%, you simply pay us
an agreed upon creative fee. Should the test results be
impressive – and we both wish to enter into a full-service
agency agreement – this creative fee will be refunded to you.

In effect, we offer you a risk-free trial of our advertising
pulling power. Our work will cost you absolutely nothing – no
creative, production or media costs – unless we beat your best
ad by at least 10%.

Are There Any Catches?

There are two:

1. You must be willing to let us create advertising we
    think will sell. Except for your legal and factual
    approval, we'd retain creative freedom. Naturally, if an
    ad isn't ours – if the copy has been rewritten or the
    layout redesigned – we can't guarantee its success.

2. You must need better advertising. If we think your
    present advertising is excellent, we'll tell you. We don't
    presume to be the only direct response agency that can
    turn out superlative work.

But if you're among the vast majority of advertisers whose ads aren't living up to their product's full potential, we're confident we can help you. And perhaps, you'd like to know more about us.

....

Again, in the end, the ad talks about its bold offer:

....

What Should You Do If You're Interested?

If you're interested in us and our unique offer, send us a proof of your best ad, or sample of your top direct mail package, plus any background literature you may have. We'll look it over and let you know shortly if we feel we can beat it by at least 10%. On the average, we feel we can beat about 19 out of every 20 advertisements currently in direct response. This may sound brash – but we back up our confidence with our own money. The best part about our "guaranteed results" offer is that you don't risk a cent.

....

Example #11

I took this offer from an advertisement written by a farmer who was selling grapefruits called Royal Ruby Red directly to customers through advertising.

In the ad, the farmer talks about in detail how he selects and delivers the best grapefruits for his customers. To buy his rare grapefruits, a customer has to take the club membership.

This is not common because most farmers choose the middleman route to sell their products to consumers. However, many of them keep complaining that they don't get a fair share.

Yet, there are a few farmers who sell premium items that are generally not available in the market. These farmers want to build their own business... make their own customer base... and, of course, want to earn more profits.

For these entrepreneurial farmers, **directly selling to customers** could be a better option.

However, if they want to sell directly to customers, they should know which way is most suitable for them. They could start their own retail outlets or hire in-house salespeople or sell through advertising, as shown in the below example.

If these farmers ever take my opinion, I would say go direct and sell through advertising.

In this issue, I've shared three examples of selling food products directly to consumers through advertising. These examples are going to be more and more relevant in the coming months and years because running brick-and-mortar stores is definitely not going to be easy and cheap. Moreover, due to Corona Pandemic, things have changed dramatically.

So, start learning how to market directly to customers... how to select a target market... how to create offers... and how to sell through advertising just like shown in the below example.

Here is the offer part:

....

When I realized that the Royal Ruby Reds were the ultimate fruit, I decided to form a club and sell only to my club members. In this manner, I can control my production to insure that nobody will be disappointed.

But before I ask you to join my club, I want you to sample my Royal Ruby Reds for yourself, at no cost to you whatsoever. Let me send you a box prepaid of 16 to 20 Royal Ruby Reds. Place four of them in your refrigerator until they are thoroughly cool. Then cut them in half and have your family sample this unusual fruit.

You decide whether or not Royal Ruby Reds are everything I say. You determine whether or not eating a Royal Ruby Red is the fantastic taste experience I promise.

You decide. I'm confident that you and your family will want more of this superb fruit and on a regular basis, too. If the four Royal Ruby Reds make you say "yes," then keep the remaining fruit. Otherwise return the unused fruit (at my expense) and you won't owe me a single penny.

But you are never going to know just how wonderful genuine Royal Ruby Reds are unless you place your order right quick.

This way you are sure to receive your package containing 16 to 20 Royal Ruby Reds for you and your family to sample. But since the supply is strictly limited it's important to place your order now.

Now suppose you do like Royal Ruby Reds – suppose you love them – can you be sure of getting more?

You surely can. By saying "yes" to my first shipment you have the privilege of automatically joining my Winter Fruit Club.

Please be assured you pay nothing in advance. But each month during the winter, I'll ship you a pack of 16 to 20 orchard-fresh, hand-selected, hand-picked Royal Ruby Reds.

Every Royal Ruby Red you receive will pass my tough tests. Each will weigh a pound or more. Safe delivery is guaranteed. This fruit is picked, packed and shipped each month, December through April.

You pay only after you have received each shipment. And you can skip or cancel any shipment, simply by telling me your wishes.

Remember, it obligates you to nothing except making a taste test of the best grapefruit that has ever been grown. And this taste test is on me!

Of course, as you can well imagine, when I say supplies are limited – I'm not kidding! There's just so many club members I can accept before I must close my membership this year.

....

Example #12

How many ways does your product perform better than others? **Can you give a guarantee on each performance factor?**

In this example, the guarantee is given on both - increase in power and gas-saving.

....

Guaranteed For Two Full Years!

Yes! You try these amazing POWER FLASH SPARK PLUGS for two full years entirely at our risk! First, test them for one full month for surging power, thrilling new driving performance, breath-taking gas-savings alone! During that very first month alone:

1. These plugs must give you up to 9 miles more per gallon instantly – or your full purchase price back!

2. These plugs must give you up to 31 more horsepower instantly – or your full purchase price back!

3. As an extra added assurance – these plugs must
   continue to give you this power, performance and gas
   savings FOR TWO FULL YEARS – or we will send
   you a brand new set ABSOLUTELY FREE!

....

Example #13

This is an excellent example of selling a premium food product through direct marketing.

You may wonder that since Olive oil is available generally in every retail store, then why is there a need to sell directly to the consumer by inviting them to become a charter member?

You see, some people are extremely concerned about the **quality** of the product no matter how much it costs. They doubt that products which are available to the masses are not so superior.

They wonder how a product which is generally grown/manufactured/developed in some other country can be so easily available in their nearby store at such a low price.

And then there are some people who are extremely sensitive to **taste**. They are desperately craving, fantasizing, dying for the original taste which they miss in their local product.

And then there are some people who can't compromise their **health**. They want purest, freshest, natural products. They hate chemicals and preservatives.

The reasons could be many, but the point is **there is always a niche market available**... people who are looking for rare/best/unique experience which they know can't be found in their local area.

If you can find such people and understand and fulfil their desire, it's no wonder you may soon become wealthy by selling to a niche market.

....

This announcement is your invitation to join us on this wonderful, ever-so-much-fun adventure in the greatest taste and health benefits that the world's freshest olive oils can bestow.

Four times a year – roughly in November, February, May and July – I travel the world, following the sun to sample hundreds of fresh-pressed olive oils right at harvest time in each olive-growing region. I pick out the top three, best of the best oils. Then I put my treasures on a jet plane and, after they land in America, have them bottled by hand and rushed right to your door by express delivery truck.

This is the kind of olive oil that the Italians "novella," though other countries don't use the same term. In every case, no matter what the region of origin, I secure for our Club Members the freshest, most flavourful and healthiest olive oils available in the world, delivered at the peak of freshness and health benefits.

So when you become a Charter Member of The Fresh-Pressed Oil Club, you can expect three bottles (you'll have a choice of two sizes) of the world's freshest olive oil to show up at your home four times a year. You will never have to expend a drop of energy, or waste a second of your precious time, in tracking down great olive oil. You will be, quite literally, one of the few people on the planet with a continual supply of just-pressed insanely fresh olive oil!

....

You can add extra features, bonuses, important information along with your main product to make your offer more attractive to die-hard fans of your products.

....

As a member of *The Fresh-Pressed Olive Oil Club* you will quickly become a connoisseur of the finest fresh-pressed olive oils from all over the world! Every new bottle will be a delicious adventure in olive oil appreciation, accompanied by the Club's tasting notes, recipes, and recommendations for use.

RSVP TODAY!

If you'd like to become a Charter Member of The Fresh-Pressed Olive Oil Club, please let me know right away, so we'll have enough time to make the arrangements with our artisanal producers in time for the next harvest and shipping dates. I'll make your life simple by offering just two options. All you have to do is pick one of the following options...

Option #1, Best Value: 500-ml Set: A large set of three 500-ml (16.9 ounce) fresh-pressed supreme extra virgin olive oil for only $124 per quarter (plus $15 shipping and handling). This works out to one 500 ml (16.9 ounce) fresh-pressed bottle per month.

Option #2, Excellent Value: 250-ml Set: A smaller set of three 250-ml (8.45 ounce) bottles of fresh-pressed supreme extra virgin olive oil for only $87 per quarter (plus $12 shipping and handling). This works out to one 250 ml (8.45 ounce) fresh-pressed bottle per month.

Whichever option you select, your oils will be accompanied by my "Pressing Report," describing the producer, olive varieties, regions, harvest and delivery details of your shipment. You will also receive our tasting notes for each oil, a game-plan for an olive oil tasting party, and suggestions for ways to enjoy each of the oils, emphasizing seasonal recipes and traditional uses.

Never a "Minimum Commitment"...

And You Can Cancel at Any Time

There is no minimum number of quarters that you must enrol for, and you can cancel your membership at any time. Moreover, every quarterly shipment is protected by our 100% money-back guarantee. Just let us know if you're dissatisfied with your selections for any reason, and you'll receive 100% of your money back for that shipment, no questions asked. So you risk absolutely nothing – unless, of course, you let this chance slip by, in which case you'll be missing the opportunity to secure your own private, continuous source of rare, fresh-pressed olive oil, so few drops of which ever reach our shores!

....

Have you noticed this closing technique?

100 meals vs. a single dinner at a restaurant!

....

This Club brings you so much dinning pleasure at such reasonable cost. Indeed, these fresh-pressed, super-healthy oils can add vibrant flavour and nutritional goodness to more than 100 meals over the next three months for less than the price of a single dinner at a restaurant!

....

Example #14

Can you buy your competitor's product for your customer?

Here's an example of a bold promise of **buying a competitor's product** for an unsatisfied customer.

....

Come in and try our health product for 30 days. If within those 30 days you don't see a noticeable improvement in your health, I'll not just refund the money you're paying me, I'll also call any of my competitors – the one you would like to try next – and personally buy you your first packet.

....

Example #15

Here's a cold call (telephonic conversation) between a self-employed accountant and a prospective client.

To take the immediate attention of the prospective client, the accountant makes a bold claim. It also shows the confidence of the accountant in his expertise.

This technique could be effective **if you're planning to crack a big account, especially the one loyal to your competitor.**

....

Hello Sir,

I want an appointment with you to show my expertise. I will take only 25 minutes of yours. In these 25 minutes, I will reveal a major problem in your finance or an opportunity to save your taxes that your current accountants, bankers, lawyers, or any other advisors are not able to find out.

If I fail, I will pay you $500 or donate this amount to the charity of your choice. Is this fair enough?

....

Example #16

Here's an example of the **lowest price guarantee offer** from a company called *evo*. The offer is mentioned on the company's website.

It's truly a bold offer. You are so confident about your pricing that you ask your prospect to look at all your competitors' prices and if they find a lower price, then come back to you, and you'll quote a lesser price than already the least price available in the market.

This technique is used when you've done your homework fairly well. You've studied all your competitors' products and pricing. You know how to compensate for the loss you're making in acquiring a new customer.

Generally, big businesses can manage to give an additional discount to kill competition. But this technique could be very effective even for small businesses, especially in these two scenarios:

1) You have multiple products and services for upselling.

2) You have a renewal business.

Lowest Price Guarantee

Price Match Policy

It's our goal to provide you with the lowest possible price. If a competitor has an item available **online** at a lower final price (after any duties, tax and shipping costs), we will beat it by 5%. Good times!

To qualify for a price match, all the following must apply.

- Same model year

- Same color

- Same size

- Same condition

- Competitor site must have item in stock

- Competitor site must be U.S. based

evo's price match policy is valid in the U.S. only. Price Match discounts cannot be combined with any other offers or promotions. All competitor pricing must be verifiable online, and approval is made at the discretion of evo staff...

(source: www.evo.com)

Example #17

I like this example simply for one reason. It's fun watching Sunski's video on lifetime warranty FAQ as well as reading its terms & conditions.

Almost all businesses use a typical legal language in their terms & conditions page. Moreover, their warranty and FAQ part is also very boring to read.

But this example is very unusual, which makes the company different from its competitors. The warranty video gives its customers a **personal touch** by amusing them and reducing their anxiety before buying.

Here are the lyrics of a funny video song, which is actually a lifetime warranty FAQ from Sunski sunglasses, as mentioned on their website.

....

Sunski Backyard Quartet

FAQ Vol. 1

Lifetime Warranty

Take 4

What do I do when I have broken my sunglasses?

Where do I go when I have busted up my shades?

Tell me what is covered under Sunski warranty?

Let me tell you pretty much about everything

I sat on my shades

(we got it!)

I fell on my face

(we got it!)

A dog ate my shades

(we got it yeah yeah)

With a lifetime warrantayayayayeah

<<music continues>>

What's the deal with our sunglasses lifetime warranty?

Your pair of Sunski sunglasses is covered under our sunglasses lifetime warranty for as long as you own them. Our lifetime warranty covers all problems related to manufacturing defects that occur during the ownership of the shades. If they break under normal use, we'll fix them or replace them for you. This warranty doesn't cover lost shades, but drop us a line, and maybe we can get you a deal.

(source: www.sunski.com)

....

It's not just their video is unusual, their terms & conditions on lifetime warranty are also a bit fun to read.

Generally, the terms & conditions part makes people a bit cautious, which could delay the buying process. But in this case, just because of the manner in which the company mentioned its terms & conditions... prospects smile, agree, and lose anxiety once they read what is not covered in the lifetime warranty.

If you're also selling online, it's very important to make your customers comfortable before buying from you. And sometimes, your **honest answers with slight humour** can win the hearts of skeptical customers, just like in this case.

Busted Frames?

Our sunglasses lifetime warranty covers frame damage that prevents you from wearing your shades: broken hinges, cracked frames, damage from running into a tree on your bike... this is all fair game to be replaced. Minor damages like scuffs and small dings are not covered, because that's a waste of perfectly good shades. We also not cover really dumb things that you may do, like backing over them with your car or melting them in a fire pit (we've seen it all).

We reserve the right to decide if your damage is covered under our lifetime warranty, but tell us a good story and we'll likely be pretty lenient...

Scratched lenses?

Our SuperLight frames are virtually indestructible, but all sunglasses lenses can scratch if you adventure hard enough. The lenses are the most expensive part of a pair of shades, which is why we're not able to provide them for free under our lifetime warranty. But we do offer replacement lenses at a practical price, so that your shades can stay on your face and out of the bin.

If you've got busted lenses, head over to our Lens Kit page. Please don't send us your shades if you've scratched lenses! If your style has been discontinued, reach out to us and we'll figure something out for you. Some styles just had to be discontinued to make room for the new – this is the way things go. Thanks for understanding!

Did you read all of the above? Do you promise you're not going to send us your scratched lenses? Or little broken bits of sunglasses put through a blender?

Perfect, submit your lifetime warranty claim.

(source: www.sunski.com)

....

Example #18

Here's an example of a **FOREVER satisfaction guarantee** from Cutco knives to their customers as mentioned on their website:

How many companies are there who can give a forever satisfaction guarantee?

Well, I think very few.

Satisfaction is a vague word.

If you ask your client, "Are you satisfied with my service?"

Then even if you've fulfilled your promise and provided the best from your side, the client will always demand more.

That's why you should define the satisfaction word in your offer, just like in the below example, where the company has mentioned important elements covered in their forever satisfaction guarantee.

....

At Cutco, we stand behind our products with a FOREVER satisfaction guarantee. We want every CUTCO customer to be satisfied customer FOREVER. The guarantee has several important elements.

Forever Performance Guarantee

If at any time you are not completely satisfied with the performance of your CUTCO product, we will correct the problem or replace the product...

Forever Sharpness Guarantee

CUTCO knives with the Double-D® edge will remain sharp for many years, but after extended use they may need resharpening...

Forever Replacement Service Agreement For Misuse Or Abuse

Should you damage your CUTCO through misuse or abuse, we will replace the item for one half of the current retail price...

15 Day Unconditional Money Back Guarantee

If at any time within 15 days after receipt of your CUTCO you are not satisfied with your purchase for any reason you may get a full refund of your purchase price by contacting CUTCO customer service.

(source: www.cutco.co.uk)

....

Example #19

You see, customers hate manipulative salespeople.

They resist aggressive salespeople.

They don't want to surrender to the dominating policies of companies.

And they don't like ifs and buts in business deals.

In fact, **every customer wants to control the sales process right from the beginning**. So, if you give them that control without any risk involved of theirs, they would definitely like to try you just like in the below example of a bold promise made by a carpet cleaning company:

....

We promise to make your carpeting look like new or we will charge no money from you!

When we come to your home to clean your carpet, first we will check the worst spot in your carpet. If you find our job satisfactory then only we will proceed further to clean the whole room.

But it doesn't mean you can't check further our work. We will charge only what you approve.

And here's our special offer for you:

 If you order today, you will get one room (same area) FREE for every three rooms cleaned.

....

Example #20

In the technology era, we want to deal with professionals who will do their best to protect us from emerging problems that we have never seen before and have the power to destroy our lives.

Since most of us don't know too much about upcoming technologies and related problems... and since we have never dealt with these high tech companies and professionals before... **so we need solid assurance that they will protect us, and if they are not able to do it they will make some arrangements for our losses.**

In such cases, a bold guarantee by hi-tech companies shows the layman customer how much confidence these companies have in their capabilities.

Here's a bold guarantee from Lifelock company that deals in the protection of identity theft.

....

Our Million Dollar Protection™ Package*

Personal Expense Compensation

We will cover you for personal expenses incurred as a result of identity theft, up to the limits of your plan.

Reimbursement of Stolen Funds

If your money is stolen due to ID theft, we will reimburse up to the amount provided by your plan.

Coverage for Lawyers and Experts

If you become a victim of identity theft while a Lifelock member, we will provide the necessary lawyers and experts if needed to help resolve your case.

* ... And up to $1 million for coverage for lawyers and experts if needed, for all plans...

(Source: www.lifelock.com)

....

Example #21

This old letter, selling insurance, is one of the best examples of **how to use fear in offer**. The offer is covered in so much detail that I have included the entire letter in this issue.

Reading this letter again and again could be great learning for every kind of insurance business and the salesperson on how to pitch their insurance policies to prospects.

I consider this sales letter a **perfectly prepared pitch**. Facts and figures, emotions, family, offer, objections... almost everything is covered in this sales letter. This is how a salesperson should prepare before giving an important presentation.

I urge you to read this sales letter every day at least two times for the next 10 days and see the difference in your sales talks.

....

Dear Friend,

This is a letter that is not like any you have ever received or I have ever written. My subject is not pleasant, but it is serious.

My subject is cancer.

One out of every four Americans will get it, according to the 1975 Facts and Figures of the American Cancer Society, despite the truly excellent work of the medical profession. In fact, 53,00,000 of us now living will eventually have cancer. This means that it will strike about two out of three American families. Families like yours. Families like mine.

Until now, there have been only two things you could do to help fight this dread disease.

1. You can be sensible about your health. Annual checkups, stop smoking, etc.

2. You can be generous, by giving freely to the American Cancer Society, among many outstanding charities.

But charity should begin at home, and now it can.

Most sincerely, I urge you to read my letter carefully. It describes a plan that helps protect you against the menace of cancer. It helps protect you against having your life's savings, and those of your family, wiped out because of the almost incredible costs of cancer care.

And yet the cost of this plan is low. In fact, if you're 54 years old or under, the monthly premium is only $2.90. And if you're 55 or older the monthly premium is only $4.70. Yet we'll pay you, no matter what your age, $33.33 a day cash ($1,000.00 a month) if you're hospitalized due to cancer. That's in addition to what anybody pays you.

You will need the money.

John Wayne had lung cancer and beat it. So did Arthur Godfrey. So have millions of others, thanks to early detection and dramatic improvements in medical techniques.

But movie and TV stars are rich. They can afford the very best care and never ask what the bill will come to. It doesn't matter when life is at stake.

Or does it?

We've designed this Cancer Expense Protection Plan because too many folks we know of recovered from cancer only to find themselves a burden to their families. And because of the enormous costs of cancer treatment, the security from a lifetime of honest work had evaporated as though it had never been there at all. Before cancer, there had been independence. Now there was almost total dependence. And their spirits, frankly, died.

You can help prevent that, if you will take just one prudent step.

As you can see, the enclosed Enrollment Form is not transferable; no one but you may use it. In addition, we've made your first month's coverage just 25¢. If you have not had cancer, then I urge you to fill in and mail us the application along with your 25¢ today. In return we will send you the policy to examine yourself, so that you can make your own independent decision about it. If you like the policy, keep it and continue your cancer protection at the rates now in effect: $2.90 a month if you're 54 or under... or $4.70 a month if you're 55 or older. However, if for any reason at all, you decide it isn't just what you need, then just return the policy to us within 15 days, and we'll return your quarter. No questions asked.

You can cancel. We can't.

Regardless of how often you have been treated for cancer, just pay your premiums on time and we can't cancel you out.

And we won't.

And remember, your rate can be changed only if there's a rate adjustment on all policies of this class in your whole state. You will be never be singled out for a rate increase, regardless of how much you've collected.

We at National Home have over 50 years of experience in the insurance business. We're currently paying claims of $35,00,000.00 a year, to policyowners, under our various life, accident, and health plans.

As a thoughtful consumer, you probably have some good solid questions to ask. I will do my best to answer them forthrightly.

What are the benefits of your policy?

1. Everyday you're hospitalized because of cancer, you'll collect $33.33 cash (that's $1,000.00 a month) paid direct to you unless you tell us otherwise. Up to a maximum of $12,000.00.

2. Every daily visit from your doctor while you're hospitalized for cancer will entitle you to $10.00. Limit: $1,200.00.

3. In-Hospital Expenses for cancer treatment up to a maximum of $2,000.00. These include reasonable and customary charges of diagnostic X-rays, operating rooms, drugs, and medicines, private duty nurses, blood and plasma (unless it's replaced by your donors), ambulances, X-ray, Radium, and Radioactive Isotope therapy.

   Another part of this benefit is well worth mentioning here. Many folks live in communities where the local hospital simply doesn't have the proper treatment facilities. If your doctor says that you must go to a hospital outside your area for special treatment, your airline or railroad fare is covered, too.

4. Your surgeon's fee will also be paid by us up to the limits shown on the schedule I've enclosed. The

maximum here, for combined surgeon's and anaesthesiologist's fees is $1,200.00. (Be sure to check the little folder carefully.)

And there is more. Suppose you need a nurse at home after a covered hospital stay? Well, if you've been hospitalized for cancer for a period of 5 days or more... and if your doctor says you must have a full-time nurse within 5 days of your discharge... then National Home will pay you $14.28 a day (that's a $100.00 a week) for as many days as you received hospital benefits – up to 50 weeks.

And as I said, this protection is now available to you for just 25¢ for your first month... and then only $2.90 a month if you are 54 or under; $4.70 if you're 55 or older.

<u>Note that, please</u>: despite the fact that all this money will be paid direct to you (unless you tell us otherwise), it is not taxable. It is not income, and the IRS has ruled that it cannot be taxed.

You may wish to cover your family, too. After all, it makes good sense because – blindly – cancer strikes the young as well as the mature.

If you decide on family protection, the single premium for your whole family (including you, your spouse and all your unmarried, dependent children from birth up to age 19) is far less than you'd expect. For example, if you're 54 or under, the total family premium per month is just $5.40. If you're 55 or older, it's $7.60 a month. That's it; that's all. Regardless of how many dependent children you have. And 25¢ covers all your insured family for the first month. (It's a sad, but true fact that leukemia – a cancer of the blood – attacks children and young adults, but seldom bothers with people like you and me. Consider this, please, as a word to the wise.)

What are the exclusions and limitations?

Just as you should thoroughly understand the benefits... you should also understand the exclusions.

1. This policy does not cover any sickness, disease or incapacity, other than cancer.

2. This policy does not cover the treatment of cancer which is first manifested or diagnosed prior to 90 days after the Effective Date of the Policy.

As for the deductible, there is none. You're covered from the very first day you enter a hospital. Even before, if you require a biopsy that's diagnosed to be cancer, or an ambulance, or even air or rail transportation, as I mentioned.

An important point is well worth repeating: we can't cancel you out, as I mentioned before. And we also can't refuse your Enrollment Form. If you haven't had cancer, your enrollment will be accepted at the rates I quoted you.

There is also a built-in grace period. If you forget to pay your premium by the due date, you're still covered for 31 days after your payment is due.

(A note to young families: all children are covered, if you choose the family plan. And if a new child is born while the policy is in force, he's covered too, right from the very beginning, at no extra charge.)

Why should I buy family coverage?

Cancer is no respecter of people... or age. Men get cancer. They're more susceptible to lung cancer than women. Women get cancer, too. Fewer of them get lung cancer, statistically, but they get breast and uterine and cervical cancer. That's why every woman should have a Pap test at least once a year. And even children get cancer. That's always surprising to people – but it's all too true. That's why family protection is important. Early diagnosis, of course, is the best single way to avoid the spread of cancer. More than 1,500,000 Americans alive today have been cured of cancer, according to the American Cancer Society.

By now my point should be clear: it costs a great deal more to treat cancer than it does to treat pneumonia or a broken leg. And yet this is all it costs you to be protected:

25¢ covers your first month. Then continue at these low monthly rates.

	Individual Protection Per Month	Family Protection Per Month
54 and under	$2.90	$5.40
55 and over	$4.70	$7.60

It's true that the war on cancer has resulted in many dramatic life-saving medical techniques, but they're terribly expensive.

Regular plans (Group, Blue Cross, Blue Shield, Medicare) simply were not designed to completely cover these high costs. Most policies are not designed specifically with the costs of cancer in mind. For example, many of these plans may not cover all the costs of –

Chemotherapy, radiation and cobalt treatments, private nursing care, special medicines, ambulances, surgery, etc.

Yet this is the extra help that can save your life, or the life of someone dear to you. But these medical techniques are expensive, and National Home wants to help you keep what you've saved.

That's why the benefits from this cancer policy are paid to you over and above what you collect from anyone else. And they're paid direct to you unless you request otherwise. You spend them as you wish.

These benefits are not taxable, nor can anyone tell you how to spend them.

After all, while you're sick in the hospital with cancer, life goes on. Expenses continue, even go up. And who is going to pay those bills? Just because you're hospitalized doesn't mean that the on-going bills stop.

There is no reason anymore to be frightened about the cost of treating cancer. For National Home is ready to help. And, as I said, it takes but one prudent step on your part.

Fill in and mail us the enclosed application today... along with 25¢. (The return envelope is postpaid.) We'll send you your policy, with an Effective Date shown on it. Read it carefully, please. If you don't like it... if you feel, for any reason at all, that it doesn't meet your requirements, send it back within 15 days of receiving it, and we'll return your money.

That's all; there's absolutely no risk on your part. Under our 15-day money-back offer, you don't risk one cent!

If you decide not to take advantage of this offer, I'll understand. But do think it over carefully. Who knows when you'll get an opportunity as good as this again?

Sincerely yours,

Arthur S. DeMoss

President

National Home Life Assurance Co.

P.S. "People are Funny," as my good friend Art Linkletter has said so often. But they're also funny about believing that cancer always happens to the "other guy". It doesn't.

Please think about it. Then send us your completed Enrollment Form.

....

Questions to Gain Agreement from Your Prospects

The mantra of successful selling is **First Convince and Then Persuade**.

Right from the first sales meeting to delivering your sales pitch to closing the deal, your major task is to gain as many verbal or non-verbal agreements from your prospect as you can.

You need to keep asking questions smartly to assure yourself that the prospect is gradually accepting your every point.

1. "Isn't it?"

2. "Won't you?"

3. "Don't you?"

4. "Can't you?"

5. "Aren't they?"

6. "Make sense?"

7. "I think I've caught you at a bad time. Would you want to discuss this proposal at a later time, or would you prefer that I continue?"

8. "Do you agree with that?"

9. "You would, wouldn't you?"

10. "What else do you need to know?"

11. "How interested are you?"

12. "You're with me on this, right?"

13. "Is that what you were looking to spend today?"

14. "Are you still interested?"

15. "Is that within your budget?"

16. "Most people, including you, clearly understand that good things are not cheap and cheap things are rarely good. You do want something you can depend on over the long period, don't you?"

17. "How willing would you be?"

18. "How does that compare with what you are paying now?"

19. "Am I correct?"

20. "You'd have to agree with that, wouldn't you?"

21. "Right?"

22. "Agreed?"

23. "Does that make sense?"

24. "And that's a nice feature, isn't it?"

25. "How would you use that?"

26. "Do you understand how that works?"

27. "Do you know why this is so popular?"

28. "What do you mean exactly?"

29. "How might this work for you?"

30. "Do you want to know how much does this house cost?"

31. "You are getting a bargain when you invest in quality, aren't you?"

32. "Tell me, would that fit into your budget?"

33. "Have you made it yet?"

34. "Did I catch you at a busy time, or do you have 7 minutes to talk?"

35. "Would this location work for you?"

36. "Isn't that right?"

37. "That's pretty good, isn't it?"

38. "What questions do you have?"

39. "That's one of our biggest selling points. Could you tell me how this impacts what you're currently doing?"

40. "How did you come to this belief?"

41. "Let me ask you, do you like the product?"

42. "Wouldn't you agree that it's not difficult to pay too much for something you really like?"

43. "Good solution, right?"

44. "Understand?"

45. "Got it?"

46. "Wouldn't it have been better to have paid the regular price for this car and gotten your favourite colour and drive it for years to come?"

47. "That's a nice feature, don't you think?"

48. "What do you think of this so far?"

49. "Do we have an agreement?"

50. "And who wouldn't want that?"

51. "Will that work?"

52. "Does this help?"

53. "Wouldn't you agree that it's better to pay a little more than you expected than a little less than you should?"

54. "How would that work for you?"

55. "I can't think of a better way, can you?"

56. "What other area are you interested in?"

57. "Do you agree on this point?"

58. "You know how excited I'm about showing our new innovation, which is the answer to your problem. And that's what you really want, isn't it?"

Objections and How to Deal with Them

Many salespeople are afraid of prospects' objections. They think if they are not able to solve prospects' queries, they may lose the sale.

Instead of worrying about objections, you should be glad because if a prospect is raising objections during your sales presentation, it means he is interested in your products and services.

In fact, answering the prospect's objections is one of the smartest ways to kill competition.

An objection is an opportunity to know what's going on in the prospect's mind.

It's an opportunity to understand the beliefs and fears that drives the prospect.

It's an opportunity to close the sale by establishing your superiority against your competitors.

After getting satisfactory answers from you, the prospect will feel assured that he is dealing with a knowledgeable salesperson who understands his business, his products very well.

The prospect will start treating you like a consultant who is there to solve the prospect's problems by giving him a perfect solution.

Remember, there are no sales without objections. Objections indicate interest.

I have seen that top salespeople are masters in dealing with objections.

In fact, top salespeople anticipate prospects' objections before even meeting them.

Different Types of Objections

Price Objection

This is the most common objection raised by prospects.

Price resistance is how a prospect tells you that you have not given him enough evidence that the benefits outweigh the price.

Remember, the higher the VALUE you create for your product, the lower the price resistance.

Here are some examples of how to deal with Price Objection.

If you're selling an expensive product, take the prospect's attention towards Quality, and explain the difference between Price vs. Cost.

Price vs. Cost Close

This technique is used when the prospect is very much concerned about the price of your product.

Here you need to show the prospect the difference between the one-time high price of a quality product and regular repair or maintenance costs of a cheap product.

Examples:

- "I agree with you that this product is not at all cheap. However, there are some reasons why it is priced high. Do you want me to explain to you why we charge what we do?"

- "Since you are so much concerned about price, let me ask you one question. Is it really price, or is it the cost you're concerned with?" Then tell the prospect the difference between price and cost.

- "Some companies can beat us on price, but when it comes to cost, we always win. Since you're so much cost-conscious, why don't you start enjoying our lowest cost products right from today?"

- "Price is a one-time thing. But Cost can go on forever, as long as you have that product. Wouldn't it be better to pay a reasonable price one time than to go on paying those little costs?"

- "Why settle for the cheap replica when in the long run, the original costs less?"

- "We may not be able to give you the lowest price but can give 24X7 tech support, which could save your projects from getting delayed. How does that sound to you?"

Quality Close

Whenever a prospect takes the discussion towards a high price, you start talking about the quality and performance of your product.

Examples:

- "We decided it's easier to explain the high price one time than to apologize for poor quality again and again. I'm sure you appreciate our decision. Don't you?"

- "Would you agree that a product is worth what all it can do for you for as long as you keep it and not what you have to pay for it?"

- "Wouldn't it have been better to have paid a little more than you thought to get exactly what you needed?"

- If the prospect tries to shorten the sales conversation by just asking about price, you say, "Is the price your only concern? Don't you want to know about superior quality, 1-year warranty, immediate delivery, and our 24X7 customer service?"

Quality Objection

It means the prospect is not sure about the quality and performance of your product.

If your price is competitive, still, you may lose the deal unless you clear the doubt of your prospect on your product's quality.

Here are some examples of how to deal with Quality Objection…

- Use testimonials

- Prospects are influenced by other people's experience with your product or service. When you assure them that others had doubts initially but went ahead and purchased your product and were happy with the results, they would like to try your product as well.

- Demonstrate the product

- Take prospect for a test drive

- Provide trial license

- Give a sample of your product

Reputation Objection

If your reputation is bad in the market, then you will always face this objection from your prospect.

The best way to deal with it is to accept this problem and keep updating your prospect (even after getting the deal) on how you and your company are working on improving your reputation.

Competitive Objection

Many salespeople are extremely cautious of competition.

They don't want to lose the deal to competitors.

That's why they reduce price, come up with super aggressive offers, and even ready to get the deal without making any profit just to kill the competition.

In all these fights customer emerges as the ultimate winner.

Nowadays, customers are very smart. They are aware of the competition and know how to take advantage of it.

There is nothing wrong with this. The prospect has the full right to thoroughly check all other competitors' offers and products and then to make the final decision. After all, it's the customer who will ultimately enjoy the benefits of your products.

But it should be a WIN/WIN deal for both parties. If you don't make a profit, you can't survive in the long run.

The best way to deal with competitive objections is by following these four steps in every sales call:

1) Build rapport with your prospect

2) Sell yourself first

3) Then your company

4) And finally, your products

Newness Objection

This objection arises when you are new in the market.

The prospect hasn't heard anything about you.

There are no references, no testimonials, and no credibility.

For a prospect, you're a stranger. In such cases, the prospect is quite afraid of making the wrong decision.

Here, since you're a small company, you have the flexibility to provide innovative and customized solutions, extraordinary service to your customer.

Also, you have an advantage against big bureaucratic companies who don't care too much about the customer after getting the deal.

Many times customers are fed up dealing with old organizations because they have so many customers that they can't pay attention to everyone.

The big companies are so much involved in their daily processes and operations that they ignore the most important person in their business - their customer - who is giving them his hard-earned money to build their empire.

Capability Objection

If your prospect has doubts about your product's capability, the best way to deal with this problem is to demonstrate how your product is capable of performing the task.

There is a famous old example of how Otis demonstrated the new automatic braking system, which could stop the elevator from falling if the cables suddenly broke.

At that time, people were extremely afraid of using elevators because of deadly accidents.

When Otis developed this new braking system, he announced everywhere about his achievement. But nobody believed him.

Otis was extremely disappointed that in spite of such a great innovation, people were still afraid of riding in elevators.

Then one day, he got one idea.

Otis himself demonstrated the capability of his automatic braking system in front of the public in New York, where he rode in an open-sided elevator and then had his assistant cut the rope cable with an axe.

The elevator dropped a few inches and then stopped securely.

This demonstration made headlines across America. The public lost its fear of riding in elevators. Only the condition was they should be OTIS elevators.

After this demonstration, developers all across the world started making buildings more than four stories high because the public no longer feared elevators.

How to Treat Objections

- The very best way to handle initial sales resistance: "That's all right. Most people felt the same way when I met them for the first time. But now they have become our best customers. They are completely satisfied with our products. In fact, they recommend us to their friends and relatives."

- No matter how tough the objection is, don't take it personally. Consider every objection as a question; as a request for more information.

- You should feel glad that the customer is asking you for a reason to do away with the price objection. Her "I can't afford it" statement really means, "Show me how I can justify spending this amount of money to my friends and family."

- The objection could grow into a monster if you don't take any action. Close it when it's small.

- If the prospect tells you that he wants to discuss this proposal with others also, he is actually asking you to give him sufficient reasons to buy now so that he doesn't need to take someone else's view.

Unspoken Objections

Sometimes the prospect doesn't tell you anything. He just listens to you but doesn't give you any feedback, without which you don't know whether your presentation is going in the right or wrong direction.

This is called unspoken objection when the prospect has concerns with your proposal, but he's not telling you.

Here your strategy is to let the prospect talk more. Ask some open-ended or test-close questions, and show your willingness to listen to their answers.

Examples:

1. "I think there must be some reason why you are still hesitating. Would you mind if I ask what that reason is?"

2. "As you can see, the price is more than fair, and the product is worth every dime we're asking. Are you ready to go ahead and take advantage of this offer today?"

3. "What do we have to do to make a deal today?"

4. "How soon do you need it?"

5. "When would you like to get started?"

6. "Do you need this right away?"

7. "How many of these would you like?"

8. "Can we get this started for you?"

9. "Do you like what I have shown you so far?"

10. "By the way, which of these two would you prefer?"

11. "This institute is getting bigger and bigger and better and better. So, why don't you join now?"

12. "How interested are you?"

13. "Are you still interested?"

14. "How willing would you be?"

15. "When would you decide?"

16. "Tell me, how close are you to deciding to move forward with this?"

17. "When would you begin?"

18. "Have you made it yet?"

19. "When would you want to start?"

20. "Why don't you give us a try?"

21. "Why don't you take it?"

22. "Why don't you buy it?"

23. "How does this sound so far?"

24. "Does this ring a bell with you?"

25. "Fortunately, this product is available at a great value today. Even I'd take as many as I could at that price. So, how many should I ship you today?"

26. "Would that be enough for you to move forward with this?"

27. "How many departments would want one of these as well?"

28. "By the way, how many extra sales would you need in order to get your entire investment back?"

29. "Suppose you find this as your dream house. Exactly like you and your wife always wanted. How much more can you invest?"

The Art of Listening

One of the best ways for salespeople to increase their closing ratio is to simply improve their listening skills.

The general rule is the time spent on listening should be twice of time spent on speaking.

But it's not enough.

The more important part is how we listen to others. Listening is an art, just like speaking. Mastering this art could do wonders for you, especially if you're into one-to-one selling.

I still remember I closed some crucial deals just because of my good listening skills. I didn't make any special effort in closing these deals. My competitors made my job easy as they were not good listeners. I'm sure they had never thought about it.

If you're anxious to know the effectiveness of your listening skills, here are some hints by which you can check whether your listening skills are not good enough:

✔ You keep on talking and talking even if your potential client is not showing too much interest.

✔ You pretend that you're listening to your customer… but actually, you're thinking about how to close this Sale.

✔ Due to excitement to show one more feature, you cut your customer's sentence before she could complete it.

✔ You interrupt or finish the sentence of your customer before she could complete it herself because you know what she is going to say next.

✔ While your customer is speaking to you, you look at your watch as you've to leave for another meeting.

✔ While your customer is speaking to you, you look here and there to see what else is happening.

✔ You start doing some tasks (like checking new messages/emails) when your customer keeps talking for a long time.

✔ When your customer is still speaking, you plan what you'll say next.

✔ You start losing patience when someone speaks very slowly. The anxiety can be clearly seen through your body movement.

✔ When your customer speaks too fast, you ignore words that you haven't listened to properly but keep nodding your head.

✔ If you can't understand your customer's accent, you don't mention it to your customer; instead, simply make fake expressions that you're listening to.

How to Improve Your Listening Skills

Here are some ways to improve your listening skills:

> **Listen with your eyes** and not just with your ears. Your customer wants to look at him directly in his eyes when you're listening to him.

> **Take a pause** (count 1 to 5) before replying to customer's queries.

> **Keep asking questions** for clarifications, which assures the customer that you're listening.

> **Use opened-ended questions** that start with What, How, Why, When, Who, Which, Where...

Examples:

- "Then what did you do to overcome that problem?"

- "Why are you still using that old product?"

- "How do you manage your daily work without this product?"

- "Who gave you a demonstration earlier? Why didn't that salesperson share all these important points?"

➢ Ask your spouse, friends, colleagues, business partners, customers, boss, elders... **how much they rate you as a listener**?

1 = Poor Listener and 5 = Best Listener

➢ **Use Close-ended questions** to show your customer that you're listening to every word.

Examples:

- "Oh! Is it true?"

- "Oh my God! Are you serious?"

- "Really?"

- "Did your idea work then?"

- "On which date are you going on holiday?"

- "Is that correct?"

➢ **Use a confirming statement** to assure your customer that you have listened properly and in case you misunderstood something, then please clarify that point again.

Examples:

- "Let me confirm what I've understood till now..."

- "I'd just like to confirm that you want..."

- "Let me make sure I fully understand your problem..."

- "So you actually want..."

➤ **Check with your customer** that your understanding is correct.

Examples:

- "Am I right?"

- "Did I get it right?"

- "Did I understand your problem correctly?"

- "That's it?"

- "Is that all?"

➤ While listening, **keep making little sounds** like hmmm, oh, huh... It assures the speaker that you're paying full attention. This becomes much more important when you're talking over the phone.

➤ **Don't answer any phone call** while listening.

➤ **Clarify any misunderstandings**.

Examples:

- "I'm not able to get this point. Could you please repeat it?"

- "I'm sorry, but I don't agree with you on the last point. Or maybe, I'm not able to understand it properly. Could you please explain in detail what you were saying?"

➤ Once the listening is over, **summarize key points** to reassure the speaker that you've listened to everything and even remember the key points discussed during the meeting.

Examples:

- "The most important criteria for you to buy is quality and not quantity."

- "My price is stopping you from buying today."

- "You want to go for the imported model if its spare parts are easily available in our country."

Forms of Listening

There are three forms of listening:

1) Reflective Listening

2) Paraphrase Listening

3) Shared Listening

Let's discuss all these forms in detail.

Reflective Listening

Reflective Listening is one of the easiest ways to build rapport with your prospective clients. Since Reflective Listening requires the least creativity, so new salespeople should start with this form of listening.

Here's how it works:

When your client ends speaking, you simply repeat some words exactly that your client used during the session.

It's just the same thing that waiters do when you order your food. Once you complete your order, the waiter repeats all the items in exactly the same sequence. It subconsciously satisfies you that you've been heard properly.

Likewise, when you repeat your clients' words, they appreciate that you're paying attention to what they're saying. They feel relaxed that at last, there is someone in this busy world who listens to what they say. They find you caring, understanding, mature, and dependable.

However, don't expect from your clients that they will share with you about how much they like you and appreciate you for listening to them. In fact, most of the time, they're not even consciously aware that why suddenly they've started liking you. It's all happening subconsciously.

Here is an example of how to adopt Reflective Listening in your daily conversations:

....

Prospect: "Right from the beginning, I've never compromised with the quality whenever I've made an important purchase. But these days it's very difficult to find out which product is right for me. So, I've to dig deep before making a final decision. I don't want to regret later for making a wrong buying decision."

Salesperson: "Yeah, I agree with you that these days it's very difficult to find out which product is right for us as there are so many choices available in the market. I've seen that many people are afraid of making the wrong decision. That's why I ask all my potential clients to visit my website first and read all my blogs, testimonials, product details before making the final decision. I don't want them to regret it later. This strategy worked really well for me."

....

So you can see that Salesperson repeated the following words of the prospect:

- "These days it's very difficult to find out which product is right for me."

- "Afraid of making the wrong buying decision."

- "Before making the final decision."

- "Don't want to regret later."

When you repeat your clients' words, your clients start feeling like they are talking to their mirror, even if they have never met you once in life and just talked over the phone.

Whom do you think people love the most?

Themselves, of course!

That's why people are always seduced by their mirror image.

Reflective Listening works extremely well when you pick and say the **keywords** used by your client frequently and unconsciously. These are ordinary words but often repeated by a particular person. Here are some common keywords that I've seen people use in their daily conversations:

- ❖ "Obviously"

- ❖ "You know"

- ❖ "Frankly speaking"

- ❖ "Honestly speaking"

- ❖ "To be honest"

- ❖ "Don't mind"

- ❖ "As a matter of fact"

- ❖ "The fact is"

- ❖ "The point is"

- ❖ "Apparently"

- ❖ "Technically"

There are hundreds of such words. When you talk to others, you may find an individual using any such words frequently in conversation. Once you pick that word, start using it in your speech and see the magic of how that person is subconsciously inclined towards you.

For example, a few years ago, I was conducting a workshop for some high-profile clients. I noticed one of the participants, the Managing Director of a big company, was frequently using the word "Logically" in his conversations. I picked that word and started using it in my sentences. This resulted in building rapport and more active participation from his side. And it also helped in getting one of the best testimonials.

There is another way to find and repeat keywords. Visual/Auditory/Kinesthetic people use different predicates in their communication. Your job is to pick those words while listening to them and start using them in your talks.

Visual people use keywords like see, apparently, show, look...

Auditory people use keywords like sound, listen, hear, speak...

Kinesthetic people use keywords like feel, understand, relax, hold...

Paraphrase Listening

Paraphrase Listening is the next level of Reflective Listening. In Paraphrase Listening, instead of repeating the same words, you paraphrase what your client has just said.

As compared to Reflective Listening, Paraphrase Listening is a higher level skill because it requires some creativity to paraphrase your client's words with different words.

The question is, why you need to paraphrase your client's words?

It's because some people don't like others imitating them in any manner. They may think you're trying to seduce them. Or at worse, they may think you're mocking them. So, when you repeat the same words, they get suspicious about your intention.

Also, some people get irritated if you overuse Reflective Listening.

In such cases, you need to paraphrase your clients' words so that you don't come under the radar of your clients' suspicions.

When you paraphrase your clients' words, they still appreciate that you're paying attention to what they're saying. In fact, they like that you're giving a broader and better meaning or summarizing what they've just said.

Here is an example of how to adopt Paraphrase Listening in your daily conversations:

....

Prospect: "Right from the beginning, I've never compromised with the quality whenever I've made an important purchase. But these days it's very difficult to find out which product is right for me. So, I've to dig deep before making a final decision. I don't want to regret later for making a wrong buying decision."

Salesperson: "Yeah, these days the market is flooded with so many cheap and inferior products that it has become tough for value-sensitive customers to find out the best fit for them. They don't like making the wrong choices. That's why I ask all my potential clients to visit my website first and read all my blogs before investing in my products & services. I don't want them to feel buyer's remorse. This strategy worked really well for me."

....

So you can see that the salesperson paraphrased the following words of the prospect:

- **Prospect:** "These days it's very difficult to find out which product is right for me."

  Salesperson: "It has become tough for value-sensitive customers to find out the best fit for them."

- **Prospect:** "Afraid of making a wrong buying decision."

  Salesperson: "Don't like making wrong choices."

- **Prospect:** "Before making a final decision."

  Salesperson: "Before investing in products & services."

- **Prospect:** "Don't want to regret later."

  Salesperson: "Don't want to feel buyer's remorse."

Shared Listening

Unlike Reflective Listening and Paraphrase Listening, Shared Listening is the most subtle form of listening, which takes place in the form of conversation. It works well, especially in those cases where clients are reluctant to answer the questions of salespeople.

Shared Listening is the best form of listening simply because your client doesn't feel he is being interviewed or interrogated by a salesperson where he has to reply to one question after another.

Shared Listening makes clients comfortable and open up in front of a salesperson.

Here's how it works:

When the client shares his ideas, feelings, or experiences, you also acknowledge his thoughts by sharing your own relevant experiences. It's just like how two friends talk with each other.

Here is an example of how to adopt Shared Listening in your daily conversations:

Prospect: "Right from the beginning, I've never compromised with the quality whenever I've made an important purchase. But these days it's very difficult to find out which product is right for me. So, I've to dig deep before making a final decision. I don't want to regret later for making a wrong buying decision."

Salesperson: "Mr. Prospect, in my sales career right from the beginning, I got many job offers, but I chose only those companies which had a strong reputation in terms of ethics and quality. Even though competitors kept trying to lure me with higher salaries and commissions... but I always thought about my customers first because of whom I'm here today. I always wanted to sell the best quality products so that my customers never feel regret for making a wrong decision."

Prospect: "You sound a bit different from other salespeople who just want to sell mediocre products and complete their monthly quotas without thinking about customers. I don't know how they survive in the long-term. First, these salespeople make big promises to us, and after some time, they join some other company. I don't know how their organizations deal with a huge employee turnover."

Salesperson: "I had a very bad experience in my first sales job, which taught me a big lesson. The customer trusted my words and purchased expensive software from my company. It was a new software, and I was also new to the company. I was not aware that the software had some technical issues, and nobody in my company was able to solve them. My customer had to suffer a lot because of this. So, now I do proper research before suggesting anything to my clients. It's not just employee turnover but also customer turnover, which cost companies fortunes."

Prospect: "So true!"

Salesperson: "Yeah, since I don't like both employee turnover and customer turnover, I ask all of them to visit my website first and read all my blogs before investing in my products & services."

....

So, you can see how the salesperson shared his personal thought and experiences to match the prospect's beliefs.

As compared to Reflective and Paraphrase Listening, Shared Listening requires much higher skill and practice to accomplish the objective of building a strong rapport with the client.

Moreover, Shared Listening has a long-lasting effect because people may forget your imitation and rephrases, but they remember your stories and experiences.

Closing The Deal

One of the biggest frustrations for an organization is not getting enough sales despite having the best products, people, and resources in the organization.

This is because salespeople are not able to close the deals even after they have done all their efforts.

And it's not only organizations who are frustrated.
Almost 1/3 rd of salespeople drop out of selling each year since they cannot deal with the rejection of prospects and pressure from management to bring sales.

Closing is often the most painful part of the sales presentation. It is the part that many salespeople dislike the most. The idea of losing the sale can be very stressful.

You start to feel tense; sometimes, your heart rate increases and your throat gets dry.

Since you are asking the prospect to take action, and if he says no to your proposal, then what will you do? By worrying about it, you develop a tremendous fear of failure inside your mind.

Let me tell you frankly, the only reason that you might be nervous about Closing today is that you have not yet mastered the process.

You need to learn how to close the deals so that you could be ahead of the game.

Once you learn Closing techniques, the less stressful it will be your experience.

Gradually, you will start Closing effortlessly because you now know how to ask the right questions at the right time.

In short, you'll become an Assistant Buyer whose job is to help the prospect to make a sound buying decision.

I want you to master the Closing process so that you never feel afraid asking the prospect to make a buying decision.

So that nobody can stop you from closing deals.

And nobody can stop you from moving from being an average sales guy to the go-getter.

Below I'm sharing with you 23 powerful techniques to close the deals.

The Assumptive Close

The Salesperson never asks specifically for approval. It is simply assumed.

You can't imagine how effective this strategy works.

You talk in a manner that the prospect is going to buy today.

You're not expecting any objections from the prospect.

Here you've created an environment to make the sale as smooth as possible without any last moment glitches.

Examples:

"If you are planning on paying through financing, then shall we go to the finance manager before he leaves for the day?"

"Now that you've test-driven the car, do you want the gear shift or automatic transmission? In red?"

Your body language plays a very important role in closing the deals.

If you doubt on prospect's intention, he will see it through your body language even if you don't express your doubts through words.

The impact of our Body Language is HUGE on your prospect.

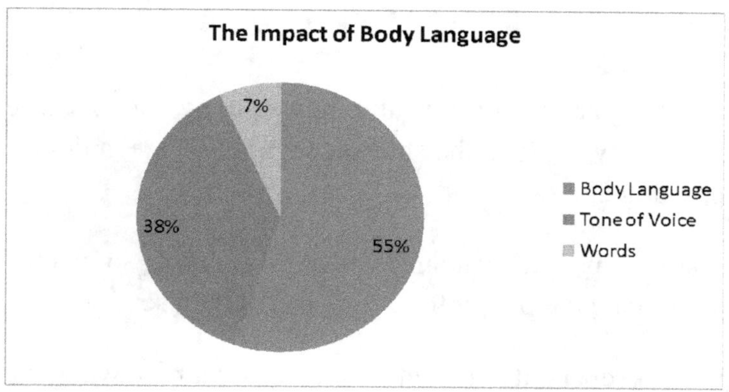

The Impact of Body Language
7%
38%
55%
Body Language
Tone of Voice
Words

The Puppy-Dog Close

Generally, parents don't want to buy a puppy dog, but when a kid starts crying, then the shopkeeper applies a technique called puppy-dog close.

He asks the parents that since the child is crying so much, it's better to take the puppy for 2-3 days and then send it back.

For shopkeepers, it's a surefire way to sell a puppy dog by letting someone take it home for 2-3 days.

Now, what happens when the puppy reaches home?

After playing with the puppy for some time, the kid gets engaged in playing other games.

But parents get busy taking care of the puppy.

Eventually, they start loving that puppy as they are feeding him throughout the day.

The puppy is sleeping in the same room with parents.

Even their neighbours start talking about the puppy. Someone says, "He is sooo cute."

The kid's friends start playing with him.

After 2-3 days, no one wants to send the puppy back to the shop.

He has become part of the family.

This technique is superb.

You can apply this technique creatively to sell your products and services.

You can send a car, bike, TV, Gym equipment, furniture to home for a few days.

You can provide trial licenses of the software, membership website, and online streaming videos.

Belief Close

I've seen many salespeople lose sales just because they don't believe in their own products.

If you want to sell your products, your customer needs to feel the same way that you feel about your product.

If you and your salespeople don't believe in your products, then how it's possible to convince your customers that you have the best products available in the market?

This is one of the main reasons many salespeople struggle in their profession, and companies die who rely on such salespeople.

Many salespeople don't agree with me when I make such a remark in my in-house sales training. They counter by saying they fully believe in their products and have no doubts about them.

And then, to prove my point, I take a small test to check how much they believe in their products.

I ask a very simple question, **"How many of you are using the SAME product that you're selling to your customers?"**

Most of the time, only a few hands go up.

Then I ask them, "If you are not using your own product, then how is it possible to ask your customer to use the product that you sell?"

Let me explain with one scenario how important this point is.

Suppose you're selling X brand bike, but you have Y brand bike at your home. The reason could be anything, like:

Earlier, you were in a different company selling Y brand bike.

Or it's not your bike. You're using your brother's bike.

Now one day, while you are riding a Y brand bike to buy some groceries from the market, you meet one of your potential customers whom you pitched X brand bike a few days back. Now, what question will come into your prospect's mind?

Gotcha!

Through this example, I want to teach you an important lesson…

It doesn't matter how good you're in prospecting, presenting, and closing… if you fail in expressing your conviction, you will lose the sale.

You see, there are three categories of belief:

1) **Opinion**: Opinion is the weakest form of belief because its intensity is very low.

2) **Faith**: Faith is stronger than Opinion because of its higher intensity.

3) **Conviction**: Conviction is the strongest form of belief because of the highest intensity. Here what you SAY and what you DO completely match each other.

So, after conducting this test, the first thing I suggest all salespeople of the company is to discard their competitor's products and start using their company's products even if it's out of their budget.

And not just salespeople, in fact, the entire staff of the company should buy and use the company's products.

If their products are high-ticket items, then the company should make some arrangements on how to finance it for their employees.

The point is, your customer will never buy your product if he doesn't see conviction at your end.

He might think you just want to sell your product to make some commission. After some time you'll switch to some other job and forget about him.

The Alternative-Choice Close

This technique is used when the prospect is a bit confused or making a delay in giving the order.

It's our job to assist our customers in buying our products. We have to find out all their objections, prepare answers to these objections, and even then also if customers are trying to procrastinate, we have to move them towards closing the deal very smoothly.

Sometimes, a Closing Question is enough to change a customer's focus towards Closing. Like, in the case of asking **Alternative-Choice Closing Questions,** which is based on the Principle of Contrast. The prospect is asked to choose between two options in the confirming process.

Just, for example, I'm sharing three ways to use Alternative-Choice Closing Questions. There could be many ways to ask such questions, depending on how creative you are.

Closing Questions to Divert Prospect's Focus on

The Type of Model

- "Would you rather take the large or medium size?"

- "Would you like the advanced version or the regular?"

- "Would you prefer the blue one or the purple one?"

Closing Questions to Divert Prospect's Focus on

The Mode of Delivery

- "Would you like to take it with you, or should we send it out?"

- "Shall I ask the company to ship it as soon as possible, or would two weeks be better?"

- "Are you in a rush, or would Wednesday be all right?"

- "Would you like delivery tomorrow or would next week be better?"

Closing Questions to Divert Prospect's Focus on

The Billing Process

- "Do you want it billed in your name or your wife's name?"

- "Would you like to have your own bank finance this, or would you like to go with us?"

- "Would you want to make a large deposit initially so that monthly deposits are smaller, or would you go with a small deposit and larger monthly deposits?"

- "Do you want us to use your credit card, or are you going to pay by cash?"

- "Would you prefer that we send the billing to your office or your factory address?"

- "Do you want to give me a cheque, or do you prefer to put it on a credit card?"

The Sharp-Angle Close

It is done when a prospect asks: "Can it does X?" Salesperson: "If it does X, do you want it?"

So, basically, you want confirmation from the prospect that she will buy if your product performs the task desired by her.

By using conditions, you are indirectly telling her that your time is equally important, and you are in the business of selling, not in free demonstrations.

It might not always work since the prospect may not like your conditional approach.

But it helps you in qualifying the prospect, especially in those cases where she is taking a lot of your time without showing any major sign of interest.

For example, if the prospect asks for some more information, then you can reply with some test-close question.

If the prospect asks, "What is your best price?" then you reply, "How soon do you need it?"

If the prospect asks: "How soon can I get this?" then you reply, "How many do you want?"

Second, it helps you in getting a commitment from the prospect that she will buy your product.

Again it is totally based on your judgment. You need to apply this closing technique cautiously.

Congratulate the Prospect

You must congratulate the prospect personally, online, or by sending a letter.

You're not congratulating prospects for buying your product. You're congratulating her on making a wise decision that she has done the logical thing.

After all, it's your customer who is ultimately the biggest winner by getting this deal.

She is going to reap benefits for years and years, whereas the commission you got in selling your product might be spent within this month.

The Contrast Close

The Contrast technique is very useful when you want your prospect to compare your product and service with others. It can be price, quality, offer validity, guarantee, warranty, etc.

Examples:

- If your prospect says, "Your price is quite high." You should immediately ask, "Compared to what?"

- If your prospect says, "You've only two years warranty." You should immediately ask, "Compared to what?"

- If your prospect says, "Sometimes, we want different features in your product." You ask, "How does your current vendor handle that?"

- If your prospect says, "Let me check with the purchasing department if we can buy today or at least within this week." You reply, "I am so glad you are purchasing now because the price will go up in 30 days."

- When you say to a prospect, "This is very competitively priced", she might not take your words seriously. But when you present a price comparison from a magazine, website, or a price list from your major competitor, there is a higher chance she will believe you.

- "Our products belong to the highest price category in this market. Still, we are selling more than ever before. Would you like to know why so many people from all over the country are buying our products even though we charge more?"

- "There are many customers like you who have thoroughly examined our product, compared it with our competitors, and decided to pay more for it, even when they could get something cheap somewhere else. Would you like to know why these customers chose us against our competitors?"

The Secondary Close

It's a smart way to turn your prospect's focus from indecision to a minor point. You make it easier for him to make a buying decision.

If the prospect agrees to the minor point of the deal, he has somehow decided to buy the entire offer.

The minor point can be colour, size, type of model, or any bonus item that he gets along with the main product.

The Secondary Close helps the customer to get relieved from the anxiety that always accompanies a buying decision.

Examples:

- "Do you want this with the factory tires, or do you prefer some other company's tires?"

- If a person is considering buying a bike, washing machine, mobile, bag, etc., use a secondary close by asking, "Would you prefer this in red or silver?"

  You have changed the prospect's focus from purchasing (major issue) to the colour (secondary issue). By confirming the colour, he has decided to buy the entire product.

- "Would you like this delivered, or would you rather take it with you today?"

You have changed the prospect's focus from uncertainty to delivery (secondary issue).

  - "Which size do you prefer?"

  - "Which colour would you prefer?"

  - "Which of these two would you prefer?"

  - "When would you like delivery?"

  - "Would you like this gift wrapped?"

The 'Do it or Leave it' Close

This technique is used when the prospect is still confused and keeps saying, "Let me think it over" or "I'm not sure."

Examples:

- "Whether you buy my product or not it's fine with me. Either it's going to make a huge difference for you, or it isn't. If it's not, you shouldn't buy it. But if it is, then why not buy today?"

- "If it's in your best interests to say yes to my proposal, I ask you to say Yes. If it's in your best interests to say no, then I simply ask you to say No. Is that fair enough?"

- "If you could convince yourself that the price is completely fair, would you have any problem to say Yes today?"

- "Do you like what I have shown you so far? If yes, then instead of delaying it further, why don't you give it a try?"

- "Yes, I know that you want to take some time. But it's a superior product at a decent price. Why don't you just take it?"

The Squeeze-in Close

With this technique, you squeeze-in the price between two descriptions of the value and benefits the customer will enjoy with your product.

This technique is very useful while writing proposals to prospects.

First, you start describing the value of your product.

Then you come to the price.

And in the last, you mention all the benefits your prospect will get by buying your product now.

Example:

"This machine, including all features, raw material, and fuel, will cost you just X amount of money per month, once it is in full operation.

Not only that, we provide complete training and 24X7 tech support to you until we are sure that you are getting full value from this machine."

The 'Why Buy/Why Not Buy' Close

Take a sheet of paper and draw a line down the center.

On the left-hand side, write 'Why Buy' and on the right-hand side write, 'Why Not Buy.'

Why Buy	Why Not Buy

In the left column, you give all the reasons why the prospect should buy your product today.

Now you go to the right column.

You start this list by saying, "One of the problems you mentioned is…" Here you mention the major objection (only one) that the prospect raised during the presentation.

Then you remain quiet and let your prospect list the other reasons why he should not buy your product.

Now you add the totals on both sides.

If you've played smartly, you will have far more 'Why Buy' reasons than 'Why Not Buy' reasons.

And then you can say to your prospective customer, "Reasons for buying my product are much more than not buying. So, why not close the deal today as I've presented all my points very logically and absolutely fairly?"

The 'Personalized Order-Form' Close

This technique is used to make the prospect consciously aware of what he is buying.

Here, you ask detailed questions in order to focus on his requirements, not on objections.

You take out an Order form and start filling it in, just as if you are making notes of his points.

Each time, the prospect gives you another detail; write it on the Order form. Soon your prospect will start noticing what you're doing.

He will realize you're listening to all his problems and needs and making a personalized solution for him. Just like how doctors listen to patients, make notes while writing a prescription.

The more information the prospect gives you, the more committed he becomes to buying the product or service at the end of the meeting.

Once the Order form is complete, ask him to check the spelling of his name.

If the prospect reads the order form carefully and makes any corrections, it's a positive sign that you're going to close the deal.

There are many test-close questions you can use while filling the Order form.

For Example:

- "By the way, what is today's date?"

- "What is your correct mailing address?"

- "Please confirm the spelling of your name?"

- "Please provide your address, credit card details, etc.?"

- "Please confirm your first name, mailing address, pin code, and telephone number?"

- "Please fill in your Date of Birth and Date of Anniversary so that we can send greetings to you?"

Limited Choice Close

Humans are naturally indecisive in nature.

When you present too many varieties of your product the customer's mind is paralyzed in deciding what to buy.

That's why give only 2 to 5 choices if possible.

By giving your customers a few limited choices, you relieve them from the anxiety of decision making.

Choices can be in the form of size, colour, taste, duration, price, quality, etc.

You might be wondering if choices create anxiety in customers, then what's the need of giving choices? Why not just focus on selling one product?

The reason is: **If you give no choice, it creates psychological reactance in customers.**

What is Psychological Reactance?

It's an unpleasant feeling, resistance, protest against people, offers, rules, and regulations that are threatening to one's freedom.

It's a feeling generated in people when someone is taking away their freedom, or limiting their range of choices, or forcing them to do only what they say.

For example: If a salesperson desperately keeps insisting you buy his product today, then what will you do?

Even if you were interested in the salesperson's product... even if you found his product best and cheapest... then also you will decline his offer. In fact, you may do the opposite of what he says.

Simply because nobody can force you when and what you should buy or not. Nobody has the right to take away your freedom of choice.

Psychological Reactance plays a very important role in our personal and professional life.

Master Persuaders love to play with Psychological Reactance. I'll cover this topic in-depth in the monthly issues of my newsletter, *Persuade and Grow Rich.*

Now coming back to the Limited Choice Close, if you don't give any choice to the customer, they will show resistance.

It's human nature to compare a product with another. It gives them the satisfaction that they have taken the right decision.

But if you give too many choices, the customer will get confused about what to buy or not.

That's why keep the focus on offering limited choices if you want to sell more.

The Ownership Close

Instead of pitching your product any further, you begin talking about ownership.

In this way, you turn the prospect's focus from saying yes or no to taking possession of the product and enjoying the benefits.

Examples:

- Explain the prospect Do's and Don'ts while using the product.

- Give the instructions to the prospect on how to use the product to get the best results.

The Consultant Close

Suppose you want to buy a new LED TV. You go to a nearby electronics retail store to casually see what's available in the market.

When you enter the store, a salesperson approaches you to know what you're looking for.

But you politely send him back saying, "We'll see ourselves. No need for your assistance." You're uncomfortable that the salesperson will keep trying to sell you even if you're not prepared to buy it today.

You move towards the section where all LED TVs are displayed. For 15-20 minutes, you keep standing there looking at TVs.

While going through these LED TVs, you find that although they are of different brands, they are quite similar to each other in appearance, price, features, and warranty period.

Also, you find that in the same price range, the top branded models have slightly fewer features than less popular brands.

So, you are confused about what is right for you.

If you buy a top brand, you will miss one or two important features.

And if you buy an unpopular brand, then you may always doubt its quality. Also, you have to keep justifying to your family and friends why you chose a less popular brand.

The reason for your confusion is that you have been presented with so many TVs but with very low contrast because of which you're not able to decide which TV is right for you.

It's human nature that you hate putting too much stress in your mind, especially in the cases of making buying decisions. To remove this stress, you keep looking for shortcuts.

The busier you are, the more you search for shortcuts, particularly in making those decisions that have low significance in your life.

When you face this situation in purchasing online, one of the most frequent shortcuts you choose is to buy the best-selling product or the product with maximum top reviews.

But when you face the same situation in a retail store, the shortcut you choose is to ask the salesperson to guide you on what is right for you.

Now the same salesperson whom you've ignored earlier is no more a salesperson for you. He has now taken the role of a consultant whose job is to understand your requirements and then suggest the best options.

The 'Now or Never' Close

This closing technique is used when the prospect is not in a hurry to buy your product.

Have you ever wondered how people really believe that the sale would expire this weekend, and prices would never be this low again?

Examples:

- "This car is the last one in stock that is both automatic and red in colour. If it goes later today, we won't get another like it in stock for the next two weeks." Two weeks seems like forever to get the car.

- "Shall we go to the finance manager before she leaves for the day? If you want it today, you should see her now."

- "I just want to say that it's a superior product which is available at a good price right now. But I'm not sure about the future. Why don't you just take it?"

The Tag-Team Close

It is used when there seems to be a difference or conflict of personalities.

Sometimes prospect doesn't like the salesperson, and the salesperson recognizes this. Maybe the salesperson doesn't like the prospect, which makes it impossible to sell.

For example, an older prospect may not like a younger salesperson, or a woman may prefer to be sold to by another woman.

As soon as a salesperson realizes that he is not able to build rapport with a particular prospect, he quickly withdraws and introduces another sales guy as "someone who is expert and knows a lot more about this product than I do."

The 'No Haggle – No Hassle' Close

Have you noticed that the process of purchasing sometimes becomes very painful, especially for senior citizens who can't travel too much… or for wealthy or top-level executives who are quite busy?

What is the latest trend in marketing?

No haggle – No hassle.

For example: In automobile marketing, because everyone pays the same price for the vehicle, the customer theoretically gets the same deal as everyone else.

The vehicles themselves are probably as good as any other, but the key selling point is "no haggle – no hassle."

The dealership could arrange all the paperwork on behalf of the customer and even deliver the vehicle to the customer's home just for little extra money.

It becomes a Win-Win deal for both dealership and customer.

The dealership wins as it gets more commission per unit. The customer wins as she does not have to face a great deal of stress.

The Shame Close

Sometimes you need to hurt your prospects when you are absolutely confident they need your products and services but using the same sentence again and again, "I can't afford this."

Examples:

- "If you can't afford to repair your car, what about the ever-increasing fuel price?"

- "As I know that you work full-time, and still if you cannot pay your insurance premium, then how will your family pay the house rent, grocery bills, and kids' school fees if you are not there to work at all?"

- "If you can't afford 500 bucks to repair your TV, then how will you be able to afford the greater expense of the new TV you're going to need much sooner?"

- "If you can't afford to protect your house from rain, won't it be even more difficult to afford the new furniture, TV, refrigerator, washing machine, and house paint after a few more rainstorms?"

- "Since you want it for a long time, could you think of any reason in this world you should not treat yourself and your family as they deserve to be treated?"

- "If you are going to live in this city and particularly in this area for the next 30 years, can't you pay that extra money to have a joyful life instead of just a normal life?"

- "Is price your only concern? Are you going to make such an important decision of your life on the basis of the cheapest price?"

The 'Feel, Felt, Found' Close

The "feel, felt, found" technique is used when the prospect is doubting your product's performance.

Examples:

- "I understand how you feel. Others felt the same way when we first talked about this new invention. But this is what they found."

- "Most people felt the same way when we first met them. But now they have become our best customers, and they recommend us to their friends and relatives. Should I share some case studies with you?"

Comparison-Affordable Technique

It is also called *Reduction to the Ridiculous close.*

It involves making your deal sweeter by breaking down the price into monthly, weekly, daily, or hourly prices so that customers can easily digest the price.

Salesmanship is all about how you change the perception of your product, price, company, services, people, competition, etc. in people's minds. *Reduction to the Ridiculous* is one of the Contrast techniques about how you present the offer in the minds of customers.

Actually, the price is the same, but in order to avoid automatic rejection by the customer once he knows the full price, we contrast the breakup price with his daily expenses.

For example, comparing the breakup price of your product with the cost of tea, coffee, cold drink, groceries, petrol, movie ticket, newspaper subscription, club membership fee, snacks, utility bills, rent, medicines, clothes, etc. on which customer spends money regularly.

The objective is to break the price down into small amounts so your customers can afford it. In this way, you're making it easy for them to buy.

Here's one example to show you how this technique works:

Suppose you're a salesperson in a car dealership. A prospect comes to your showroom who wants to buy a $17,000 car. She has already arranged for money. It's a cool deal where you have to just complete formalities and deliver a car to her as soon as possible.

You request her to sit in the waiting area while you do all the paperwork.

But she prefers to see other cars in your showroom to kill time.

Within a few minutes, you notice that she is staring at a recently launched $22,000 model. She is paying attention to every detail. She is checking interiors, engine, front and backlights, and even shows interest in taking a test drive.

You suggest to her to buy this model if she is so interested.

After thinking for a while she says no as the price of this model is $22,000, whereas she is having a budget of $17,000. Although she is going to use a new car for at least 5 years, an extra $5,000 is too much for her.

Now here's a small test for you to check your salesmanship.

If you think of yourself as a customer-oriented salesperson who always thinks about the best interest of your customer then what will you do? Convince her to buy a $22,000 car or sell a car in a $17,000 budget?

Where is the salesmanship? In selling $22,000 car or selling $17,000 car?

You see, most salespeople would like to sell the customer a $17,000 car.

Why?

First, she is financially qualified for $17,000. And she already made her mind to buy that car. So, why to confuse her?

Second, salespeople are afraid that if they try to change customer's focus from the $17,000 model to some other model, they might lose the sale.

Well, my views are different.

Suppose the customer buys a $17,000 car from you. Now for the next few days, she enjoys driving her new car. And she has almost forgotten a $22,000 model.

But one day, she sees that $22,000 model parked outside her office. She comes to know that her colleague has bought it. She congratulates her colleague and reveals she also wanted to buy the same car, but due to financial constraints, she couldn't buy it.

Her colleague says she was also planning to buy a cheaper car. But then she thought she is going to drive a new car for the next 3 to 5 years, and if she doesn't buy her favourite car, then every day she will blame herself for making the wrong decision.

After listening to her colleague, your customer starts regretting not buying a $22,000 car.

And somewhere in her mind, she blames you for not convincing her to buy this new model.

Now my some tough questions for you…

First, don't you think by just getting the sale, you turn your new customer into an unhappy customer who will never buy from you again?

Second, if your customer had a budget of $17,000 to buy a new car, then she could have purchased from anywhere… from any other dealership… heck, even online. Then what's the use of you? What's your role in selling? Why does your dealership need to hire and retain people like you? You're just working as a clerk to complete the formalities… NOT as a salesperson.

Third, ask yourself, where is the real salesmanship? If you think you did right in selling a $17,000 car, then I don't agree with you. Because from my point of view, you did NOTHING. Your customer was already sold on a $17,000 car. The real salesmanship was selling in $22,000 car, which your customer fantasized about owning and driving.

Fourth, in this case, your customer's **need** was $17,000 car. But her **want** was a $22,000 model. If you focus on selling needs, then sorry to say, pal, you'll never become rich, if you're in the profession of Sales. Top salespeople are always interested in selling wants. **The real skill is converting Want into Need.**

Fifth, suppose you get a chance to correct your mistake. Instead of selling a $17,000 model, you convince her to buy a $22,000 model. My question is: What's the actual sale done by you if she agrees to buy a $22,000 model?

Think about it.

Think…

Think…

It's $5,000.

Yes, the actual sales done by you is only $5,000.

The reason is: Your customer was already sold on $17,000 before entering your showroom.

It was that extra $5,000 where she needed your help to convince her. Of course, you can't expect from your customers that they will ask you to convince them. It's your job to read their mind, particularly their unconscious signals.

In this case, your only job was to make your customer accept that $5,000 figure in her mind.

How?

By using the Comparison-Affordable technique, reduce that monster figure into a ridiculous amount.

Here's how it works:

Suppose your customer is going to use this new car for at least 5 years.

Step 1: Now divide this extra $5,000 price by 5 years, i.e. $5,000/5 = $1,000 per year.

Step 2: Divide $1,000 by 12 months, i.e. $1,000/12 = $84 per month (in round figures).

Step 3: Divide $84 by 30 days, i.e. $84/30 = $2.80 per day.

Closing Question: "Ms. Prospect, can't you spend $2.80 per day for your desired car? It's even less than what you pay for a cup of coffee."

Just see the comparison of $5,000 against $2.80, which is quite affordable for your customer.

So, by using the Comparison-Affordable technique, you're reducing price resistance by breaking the price down to its lowest common denominator. (For example, instead of saying to your customer that one-year membership will cost you $600 plus tax plus shipping, you can say that price is even less than $70 a month.)

And then, simply compare the price of your product and service with a daily cup of coffee OR bottle of beer per week OR dinner out one night per month.

Compare your price to something that your customer consumes on a regular basis.

The 'Add-on Accessories' Close

Suppose you go to a reputed mobile store to buy an expensive mobile handset.

Once you finalize the model and move towards the billing counter, the salesperson or her colleagues want to show you something else that you may like.

For example:

- ✔ High quality mobile cover

- ✔ Bluetooth headphone

- ✔ Scratch-resistant screen protector

- ✔ Wireless earphone

- ✔ Antivirus software

- ✔ Extended warranty

Of course, these are all mobile accessories that you may require as you have purchased a new handset.

But the question is, why have they not pitched you the entire package at a time?

Why are they bringing these items separately? In a big store, each of these items may be pitched by a different salesperson.

Why are they not focusing only on selling mobile handsets?

Let me answer the last question first.

One of the rules in Selling is to increase the order value (also called cart value in online shopping) as much as possible because we don't know when this new customer will come back again to our store (or website) to buy something else.

As you already know…

It's very difficult to attract new people.

It's very difficult to convert strangers into customers.

It's very difficult to sell our other products to new customers.

And it's very difficult to bring the existing customers back to our website or shop.

That's why when you get a new sale; always try to increase the order value to make more money.

This is one of the fastest ways to cover your marketing and advertising costs and even reduce the break-even time.

Referring back to the above example… Since you've already bought a mobile phone, and are not interested in buying more handsets... so the best way to increase the order value is by selling you mobile accessories.

Now coming to the first and second questions, the answer is… if the salesperson tries to sell you all accessories along with a mobile phone as a comprehensive solution, it naturally increases the total cost in your mind, which could increase your anxiety and delay your buying decision.

But the salesperson knows you're a superhot qualified case since you've just bought an expensive mobile phone and still you're inside the store.

So, she uses the **Add-on Accessories technique** to sell other items. This closing technique is used just after the main product is sold.

The objective is to bring up the extras INDEPENDENTLY of one another so that each small price seems INSIGNIFICANT… when compared to the already bought larger one.

Here are some examples where you can use this closing technique to increase your order value:

Example #1: **Retail Clothing Store**

Suppose a man enters a fashionable men's clothing store and says that he wants to buy a three-piece suit and a pair of shirts.

If you are the owner of that store, what would you show him first to make him likely to spend the most money?

The trick is to instruct your sales team to sell the costly item first.

Sell the suit first, because when the time comes to look at shirts, even expensive ones, their prices will not seem as high in comparison to the price of a three-piece suit.

The price of a three-piece suit sets an Anchor in the mind of the customer.

If you pitch him an expensive shirt first, he might shy away from spending so much money on a shirt… but if he has just bought a three-piece suit, which is obviously much more expensive than a shirt, the price of the shirt does not seem excessive.

The same principle applies in buying other accessories like a tie, belt, socks, etc. to go along with his new suit.

Example #2: **Restaurants**

Restaurant waiters normally take your entire meal order first, and once you're done, add on dessert requests.

If the price of dessert is a bit costly as compared to other nearby restaurants, still you'll find it cheap if you compare it with the expensive meal you just had.

Example #3: **Automobile Dealerships**

If you're a salesperson in an automobile dealership, what to do once the new car is sold?

Start adding accessories options like a car cover, seat cover, FM Stereo, GPS navigator, sunshades, tire inflator and pressure gauge, extended warranty, vacuum cleaner, car freshener, Bluetooth, air purifier, glass cleaner, car shampoo, etc.

The trick is to sell these accessories independently to each other.

For example, once your customer has purchased the $20,000 car, she may find it worth spending a few hundred more for deluxe rust proofing.

These are a few common examples to show you how to increase order value once your main product is sold.

In your case, you need to brainstorm with your team what accessories you can add to your business to maximize cart value.

This technique works equally well in the service industry.

The Overwhelming Close

The Overwhelming Closing technique is based on the Principle of Reciprocity.

The purpose of this Closing technique is to provide so much material/favours/information to your prospects that they feel overwhelmed and buy from you in order to reciprocate your favours.

There are various ways through which we can apply the Overwhelming Close on our prospects. Here are some of them:

1. Provide lots of information in your sales presentation, website, advertisement, etc.

2. Conduct free webinars and podcasts on different topics.

3. Conduct Questions & Answers sessions for interested people. Here you get the chance to answers all their queries and book orders.

4. Share your knowledgebase & resource library.

5. Offer free accessories along with the purchase of the main product.

6. Spend a good amount of time with your prospects.

7. Give free bonuses along with the purchase of the main product.

8. Offer Warranty/Guarantee on your products and services.

9. Offer free trials.

10. Do customization for your potential clients.

11. Offer free sample/ test drive/ beta program.

12. Share articles/blogs/daily tips on your website/emails.

13. Give free demonstration at client's place (take as much time as possible to satisfy your prospect completely).

14. Provide Do-It-Yourself tutorials and kits for product repairs.

15. Organize special trainings for customers from time to time.

16. Offer free installation and service.

17. Provide add-on plug-ins.

18. Provide in-built templates.

19. Give more quantity at the same price instead of giving a discount.

20. Provide access to analysis/statistical tools like graphs, charts, diagrams, calculator on your website.

21. Provide access to previous projects, research data, case studies, customers' feedback.

22. Share Industry/Insider/Technical Reports.

23. Send weekly newsletter.

24. Show Infographics on your website.

25. Share personal recipes to loyal customers.

26. Free evaluation & quote in case of selling highly specialized or customized service.

27. Conduct interviews with industry experts and share with your audience.

28. Provide transcripts of videos.

29. Share your list of favourite resources to gather information.

30. Share your swipe file.

31. Conduct free coaching/consulting sessions.

32. Provide free cheatsheet/checklist/special report to website visitors.

33. Conduct survey/quiz/test/inspection along with suggestions for improvement.

34. Do a pilot project/proof of concept/prototype for your potential client.

35. Build an online customer community where customers from worldwide interact with each other and share ideas and information.

36. Share progress reports of customers with them periodically.

37. Provide a free sample kit of some major products (It's a common practice in the MLM industry).

38. Keep sharing informative posts on social media.

39. Share important articles, news, emails, cut-out sections of newspapers & magazines with your clients.

40. Help your clients with their important projects.

41. Offer some solution to personal and professional problems, no matter how small your solution is.

42. Write informative advertisements and promotional messages so that your prospects get the chance to learn something from your ads always.

In business, remember that whatever favours you do for your clients should be perceived as valuable to them. Otherwise, it's of no use.

For example, suppose you're running an advertising agency, and your job is to create campaigns for your clients, which could help in increasing their sales. But instead of providing new creative ideas to your clients, you send greeting cards... invite them for lunch... entertain them... all these favours don't bring too much value for them. Such small favours may help you to get more business for the short-term… but in the long-term, only those favours, which are perceived as valuable to your clients, will help you to retain them.

Remember, the more valued help you provide to your prospects and customers, the more overwhelmed they feel, and more pressure will be created on them to do something in return for you.

Detecting Prospects' Buying Signals

Here are some signs to alert you that the prospect is almost ready to buy. Be ready to close the deal.

1. The prospect starts talking faster. He gets excited and becomes more positive.

2. The customer becomes friendly with you. He seems to relax, calm, informal, and starts asking you some personal questions.

    Examples:

    *   "How long have you been in this city?"

    *   "In which school do your kids study?"

    *   "What do you think who will win the election in your area?"

    *   "Business is quite slow these days. What about your company?"

- "Would you like another cup of coffee?"

- "What do you think who will win the world cup this time?"

3. Chin rubbing, touching you on shoulders, doing the calculation on paper are some other signs that the prospect is approaching a buying decision.

4. The prospect asks you to tell exactly what he gets with the purchase.

   Examples:

- "I've never had this particular size. What do you think? Does it look good?"

- "Are there any hidden costs?"

- "I always wanted this model. Can you please tell me what accessories are included in this?"

- "How long is the warranty?"

- "Is it easy to install?"

- "When I have to pay the first installment?"

- "Are spare parts easily available?"

- "How much is the down payment?"

- "How long does it take generally to get delivery?"

- "Do you give a guarantee also?"

- "Do you provide 24X7 tech support?"

5. Out of all these, the most common buying signals are when the prospect asks about price, terms, and delivery.

   Examples:

- "How much does this cost, exactly? Can you give me the price break-up?"

- "What sort of terms can I get on buying through a credit card?"

- "How will you deliver all editions if I decide to buy it today?"

6. Any noticeable change in behaviour, body language, or voice shows strong buying signals.

7. If the prospect sits up straight while talking to you and begins calculating numbers related to your proposal, be ready to close the deal.

8. Whenever you see a sudden change in prospect's manners or position - moving inside the room, joking, or becoming friendly - you are getting near to closing the deal.

9. Whenever a prospect asks for detailed information about the expected results or long-term benefits she will get from your service, you are moving toward closing the sale.

What Closing Questions Should You Ask?

As you know, in the sales profession, there comes a time where the sales need to be closed. Unfortunately, our customers won't always easily decide to buy.

Sometimes customers are confused.

Sometimes customers are feeling anxious.

Sometimes customers want to procrastinate buying decisions.

At those times, we need to keep asking Closing Questions using different ideas so that customers don't lose their focus from closing the deal.

Second, Closing Questions help us in qualifying serious customers.

Third, Closing Questions help us in checking whether we are moving in the right direction to close the deal or not.

Asking Closing Questions at the right time, at the right place, using the right tone and body language is great art that, once you master, could bring you tremendous results.

Moreover, if you start incorporating Persuasion principles and techniques in your Closing Questions, you could outsmart every other competitor in your industry.

Have you ever checked how many sales you have missed just because you didn't ask a closing question?

Is it too many? Ah! It's bad!

But you're not alone...

Many salespeople are afraid of asking Closing Questions. Because they are afraid that customers may say NO.

Instead, they keep increasing their pipeline...

Keep engaging in pre-sales activities...

Keep fulfilling the demands of prospective customers...

And keep working as a courier boy by delivering proposals, samples, company gifts hoping one day the prospective customer will call them and place the order.

And then during one of their sales visits, they come to know that their prospective customer is now an existing customer of their competitor.

Finally, one more name is cut from the months-old pipeline.

The point is:

Always ask for the order even if you don't know how to sell.

Just because you asked for an Order is sometimes a sufficient reason for a customer to buy from you.

Customers love to procrastinate their buying decisions even if they like your product and service.

That's why being a salesperson it's your job to close the deal.

But the question is what questions you should ask to close the deal?

In this chapter, you'll find 175 hard-hitting closing questions that you can use to close one sale after another without any fear.

You should keep these questions in your arsenal and use them whenever you get a chance.

Don't consider them just questions. They are creative ideas that you can apply whenever and wherever you get the opportunity – whether it's a face-to-face meeting, or talking on the phone, or writing an email, or selling through your ads and website.

1) "What do we have to do to make a deal today?"

2) "Can we meet next Wednesday at 3 pm, so that I can show you an outline of how we are going to work together?"

3) "How far apart still are we?"

4) "I have answered all your queries to your utmost satisfaction. Is there any point left that would cause you to hesitate about going ahead right now?"

5) "If my ideas increase your business, I'm sure you would buy more of my products. Is this a fair exchange?"

6) "You know everything you need to know to decide right now. Why don't you just take it?"

7) "If you could spread the payments over an extra 2 years and get them down below 1,000 bucks per month, would you take it?"

8) "Let's assume I get the price clearance from my company as per your terms. Would you buy it?"

9) "If you like what I have shown you so far, will you then authorize this contract?"

10) "Which colour would you prefer?"

11) "If you found something that covers all these features, would you want to get started right from today?"

12) "That's a good choice. Why don't you buy it?"

13) "Why don't you and I meet with my boss?"

14) "Why don't you just lease my product for the next
month and continue to use it as if it were your own?"

15) "Would you like to take the large or medium size?"

16) "As you can see, there are a few lines at the bottom of
this page. Would it be fine with you if I put your name
and address on those lines to confirm you that you
finally took action to get this product you desired for a
long time?"

17) "Would you go with the deluxe or the regular?"

18) "Whom do you want me to talk to next?"

19) "If I could get you a similar kind of thing but at a two-
thirds price, would you take it?"

20) "That kicks out the only hurdle between you and
ownership of the product, doesn't it?"

21) "Would you prefer one-time payment or six-month
installments?"

22) "Why don't you make the decision right now? We can
wrap it for you and load it in your car. Or we can
deliver it to you tomorrow morning."

23) "If you can spend thousands on lunch with your colleagues in restaurants, don't you think your wife deserves a beautiful kitchen for cooking, storing, and cleaning?"

24) "How will the final decision be made after the committee meets tomorrow?"

25) "Generally, how do you handle Purchase Order terms?"

26) "There seems to be some confusion in your mind that's causing you to hesitate to move further. Do you mind if I ask what it is?"

27) "Let me know which of these two would you prefer?"

28) "We're almost sold out of this model. Let me check if we can get this model in the size you want. Could you wait here for two minutes?"

29) "Could we start your subscription plan with 3 months, or would you go for 1 year and 25% discount which goes with it?"

30) "Why don't I do an online presentation for your top management if they still have queries?"

31) "Let me check with my manager and see if we can arrange immediate delivery? Could you wait at reception for a few minutes?"

32) "Did you get a chance to talk to your boss about what we discussed last time?"

33) "Just because you didn't have the chance to get this
product earlier does not mean that you should continue
to deny yourself and your family the benefits of it for
the rest of your life. What do you say?"

34) "I'm sensing that there is an issue somewhere. Where
did I go off track?"

35) "Have I covered everything? If yes, then let me know
how soon would you need this?"

36) "If you just go ahead and sign this agreement, we can
get the process started immediately so that your project
doesn't get halted anymore. That's what your major
concern is, isn't it?"

37) "Would you like to take it with you, or should we send
it out?"

38) "Shall I ask the company to ship it to you as soon as the
product reaches our warehouse?"

39) "If it costs you a thousand bucks but does you a 50
thousand worth of good, then don't you think you've
bought a bargain?"

40) "Do you want it billed in your name or your wife's
name?"

41) "If I could get it for you by tomorrow, would you take
it?"

42) "What is the correct spelling of your last name as I have to mention it in the Order form?"

43) "Would you like to have your own bank finance this, or would you like to go with us?"

44) "Would you want to make a large deposit initially, so the monthly deposits are smaller, or would you go with a small deposit and larger monthly deposits?"

45) "Do you want to use your credit card, or are you going to handle it by cash?"

46) "Would you prefer that we send the billing to your office or your residential address?"

47) "Yesterday evening, I discussed your requirement with my Boss. What we think either this is the best solution for you, or it's not. So, let's make a decision right now. What do you say?"

48) Let me know who is going to finalize this deal? You or your boss?

49) "Please confirm your first name, mailing address, PIN code, and telephone number?"

50) "Has anything changed since our last meeting?"

51) "When would you like to make advance payment?"

52) "Today morning, my boss said to be prepared for getting fired if I don't come back with the order. Now

Mr. Prospect, it's up to you. Are you releasing your Purchase Order today? If not, will you hire me?"

53) "Do you really want to lose this lucrative deal?"

54) "If you seriously want to earn 3 times more money, don't you think today is the best time to start learning this skill?"

55) "Generally, how do you handle the invoicing part?"

56) "Do you want to give me a cheque, or do you prefer net banking?"

57) "As you can see that the product meets your needs and is easily within your price range... do you want me to install the equipment right away?"

58) "If I could demonstrate to you that it's perfect for your office and give you a 1-year guarantee on that, would you take it?"

59) "Do you want me to bring it to you, or are you going to come over to my office and get it?"

60) "Did my boss do something wrong in the presentation?"

61) "What do you think we should do next?"

62) "I think I've caught you at a busy time. Let me know, would you be available tomorrow to discuss this proposal, or should I wait outside?"

63) "Have you convinced yourself, or should I tell you
more?"

64) "Are you in a rush, or would Wednesday be fine?"

65) "Generally, how do you handle pricing issues?"

66) "Sorry, but my boss was called home on an emergency,
and he's not coming back until tomorrow morning. I'm
worried; would you be able to sleep tonight not
knowing whether or not you're going to be the owner of
this beautiful house if you still stick to your old offer?"

67) "Just between you and me, what do you really think is
going to happen here?"

68) "When should we start working with your team?"

69) "Why don't we get your engineers together with mine?"

70) "Do you want this with the factory tires, or do you
prefer some other company's tires?"

71) "Is this product/service what you are exactly looking
for?"

72) "What do you think your boss will think about what
we've put together?"

73) "If I show you my new plan that could save your
company a great deal of money in the next 3 years, are
you in a position to take the decision now?"

74) "Do you need to consult with your parents before you place the order?"

75) "Would you prefer this in black or blue?"

76) "Isn't it better to pay a little more than you expected to get exactly the same thing that you're looking for?"

77) "If we could give you a written guarantee of satisfaction, would you buy this today?"

78) "If you're seriously interested in saving your hard-earned money, when do you think would be the best time to start?"

79) "Have you ever thought how much extra money you could make per month if you join our course now instead of waiting two more years?"

80) "Whether you buy my product or not it's fine with me. It's going to make either a huge difference for you or it isn't. If it's not, you shouldn't buy it. But if it is, then why not buy today?"

81) "Would you like this item to be gift wrapped?"

82) "Do you want this to be divided into 4 or 8 sections?"

83) "Would you like this delivered, or would you take it with you in your car?"

84) "If it's in your best interests to say yes to my proposal, I ask you to say Yes. If it's in your best interests to say

no, then I simply ask you to say No. Is that fair
enough?"

85) "I'm sure you're going to use this product lifetime. So,
instead of keep delaying it, don't you think you must
start enjoying the benefits now?"

86) "What do you think will it work for you?"

87) "Do you want a single piece, or would you like to go
for 5 at a 20% discount?"

88) "If you could convince yourself that the price is
completely fair, would you have any problem to say
Yes today?"

89) "Are you saying that you will go no more than the X
amount?"

90) "I know that you may go out and check other prices.
But why put yourself through that trouble? You're
probably going to end up back here anyway."

91) "Do you like what I have shown you so far? If yes, then
instead of delaying it further, why don't you give it a
try?"

92) "Yes, I know that you want to take some time. But it's a
superior product at a decent price. Why don't you just
take it?"

93) "By the way, what is today's date? I just need to fill this
sheet."

94) "If this is the only feature you are looking for, then I think you should own this machine. Shouldn't you?"

95) "Would you want us to get started on this right from today?"

96) "We may not be able to give you the lowest price but can give 24X7 tech support, which is not available elsewhere. How does that sound to you?"

97) "What if we could spread the payments over 4 years instead of 2 years? Would you be able to handle that?"

98) "I feel as if I'm missing something in this negotiation. What do you think I'm missing here?"

99) "Why don't you and I meet with our technical expert?"

100) "You do want the best product at the best price, don't you?"

101) "Please confirm the spelling of your name in order to create your account in our system?"

102) "Generally we can have this product delivered to our customer in 2-3 weeks. But if you want, I can push them to deliver in just 1 week. Should I check with my boss on this?"

103) "How much capital do you normally commit to such big deals?"

104) "Since the item is not available in our warehouse, would you be willing to book it today and wait for 2 weeks for direct delivery to your home?"

105) "We haven't heard from you in a while. Did we do something wrong in our last meeting?"

106) "Why don't we get my boss to meet your boss to finalize the deal?"

107) "If I can completely assure you that this is the right product, at the right time and at the right price, are you prepared 100% to give me an order today?"

108) "Please fill in your Date of Anniversary and Date of Birth so that we can send greetings to you?"

109) "Just between you and me, what do you think the result of the purchase committee meeting is going to be?"

110) "Given all the details of this investment, would you be in a position to make a quick decision?"

111) "Shall we go to the finance department before the manager leaves for the day? If you want it today, you should see him now."

112) "If we accept your offer, would you be ready to go ahead?"

113) "Do you have any friends I should talk to about our new product?"

114)   "I just want to say that it's a superior product which is available at a good price right now. But I'm not sure about the future. Why don't you just take it?"

115)   "I get the feeling that you are not too happy with what I've proposed here. Am I right?"

116)   "When we install this equipment at your building, would you like me to demonstrate the major features again?"

117)   "If you can't afford to repair your car, what about the ever-increasing fuel price?"

118)   "What do you think the number was going to be?"

119)   "Let me ask you one question before I meet my boss. If in case we accept your offer, are you prepared to take this product home with you right now?"

120)   "As I know that you work full-time, and still if you cannot pay your insurance premium, then how will your family pay the house rent, grocery bills, and kids' school fees if you are not there to work at all?"

121)   "Can you and I meet with your boss next Thursday at 4 pm?"

122)   "Is the price of this product out of your financial range?"

123)	"If you can't afford 500 bucks to repair your TV, then how will you be able to afford the greater expense of the new TV you're going to need much sooner?"

124)	"Why don't we set up a meeting so all four of us can go over the final plan together?"

125)	"If I share some ideas with you, which I believe could increase your business, would you be willing to go ahead with us?"

126)	"Does this make sense to you so far? Now, what is the next step?"

127)	"When you say you'll pay X amount, that's all the agreement I need. Your word is your bond for me. Am I right?"

128)	"Since you want it for a long time, could you think of any reason in this world you should not treat yourself and your family as they deserve to be treated?"

129)	"Since you can acquire this product for just X amount today, to cover all production and shipping costs, don't you think it's more than fair?"

130)	"Please help me out. What was the real reason you decided not to buy today?"

131)	"If you are going to live in this city and particularly in this area for the next 30 years, can't you pay that extra money to have a joyful life instead of just a normal life?"

132)   "This is what we're proposing. It makes sense to me. What about you?"

133)   "This policy will cover you 24 X 7, regardless of where you are and what you're doing. That's the kind of protection you want for your family, isn't it?"

134)   "Do you need this right away?"

135)   "Is price your only concern? Are you going to make such an important decision of your life on the basis of the cheapest price?"

136)   "How are you planning to pay for it?"

137)   "Is the price too much for you and your family?"

138)   "Most people in your situation felt the same way when we first met them. But now they have become our best customers, and they recommend us to their friends. Should I share some case studies with you?"

139)   "What would it take to satisfy you on this point?"

140)   "Did I do something wrong in the proposal?"

141)   "Do you think all of my customers made a mistake by investing in this product, which saves their time and money?"

142)   "How soon do you need this?"

143)   "What if we trade our new product with your existing product so that you can start using it right from today with some little extra cash?"

144)   "Should I consider your silence as consent to go for it?"

145)   "You seem to be leaning toward black, or do you prefer it in red?"

146)   "Are we thinking along the same lines in terms of features and price?"

147)   "If you can't afford to protect your house from rain, won't it be even more difficult to afford the new furniture, TV, Refrigerator, Washing Machine, and house paint after a few more rainstorms?"

148)   "When would you like to start working on this?"

149)   "Tell me frankly, what were you expecting?"

150)   "Wouldn't it be a tragedy if the only thing holding you back from earning 3 to 5 times what you're currently earning is the solid information contained in our monthly newsletter?"

151)	"What do you think? Is the price too high or too low?"

152)	"How many of these would you like to buy today?"

153)	"I think I've covered everything you asked. Let me summarize the major points, and then you can make a decision one way or the other. Fine?"

154)	"Do you like what I have shown you so far? If yes, then, why don't you give it a try?"

155)	"Thank you for asking. Yeah, sure. I will have another cup of tea. And by the way, how soon would you need this?"

156)	"Why don't I set up a conference call so you can talk to one of my customers?"

157)	"Should I mark this one SOLD while we discuss how to finance it as per terms suitable to you?"

158)	"Does our idea appeal to you?"

159)	"Don't you think it's sensible to invest in equipment which will give you trouble-free operation for the lifetime of the product?"

160)	"Is this the only thing which stands between you and ownership of this product? Or is there something else you want to discuss?"

161)   "If I do this, do we have a deal now?"

162)   "What do you think, are we having a fair exchange?"

163)   "There are many customers like you who have thoroughly examined our product, compared it with our competitors, and decided to pay more for it, even when they could get something cheap somewhere else. Would you like to know why these customers chose us against our competitors?"

164)   "Please help me out. Did I do something wrong in today's meeting? If I did, what was it?"

165)   "Tell me frankly; is the price beyond your reach?"

166)   "Our products belong to the highest price category in this market. Still, we are selling more than ever before. Would you like to know why so many people from all over the country are buying our products even though we charge more?"

167)   "Is the Purchase Order issued from your department?"

168)   "If these are only two models available in the market, which one are you going to choose?"

169)   "Out of these three, which size do you prefer?"

170)	"What if we could extend payments up to 1.5 years instead of the usual 1-year period resulting in lowering your monthly payments?"

171)	"Would you like to get it delivered to your office or your factory?"

172)	"What if I add this feature also in your package? Now can we have this deal today?"

173)	"Please provide your correct name, address, credit card details in the below order form?"

174)	If the price is so vital for you, then what about the quality of the product, warranty, and after-sale service?

175)	Do you really think our major clients would continue to pay us if our services did not pay off?

Referrals

A referral is worth 10 times a cold call.

This means that it takes 1/10 the time, energy, and resources to close a sale with a referral than it takes to start cold-calling and finding new prospects.

The fact is the highest-paid salespeople work on the basis of referrals mostly.

In the case of Joe Girard, who is considered the world's greatest automobile salesman and who sold more than 12,000 cars, out of 10 sales, 6 were from existing customers.

It's the daily task of top salespeople to ask for referrals from everyone, and everywhere they go, even on holidays.

They have developed so many sources of referrals that they leave it on junior salespeople to do cold calls.

The opposite of Referral sales is Customer Turnover. It means your existing customers are leaving you to buy from somewhere else.

They don't want to continue with you.

They are no more loyal to you.

They don't give you repeated orders.

Studies have shown that there are six reasons for customer turnover…

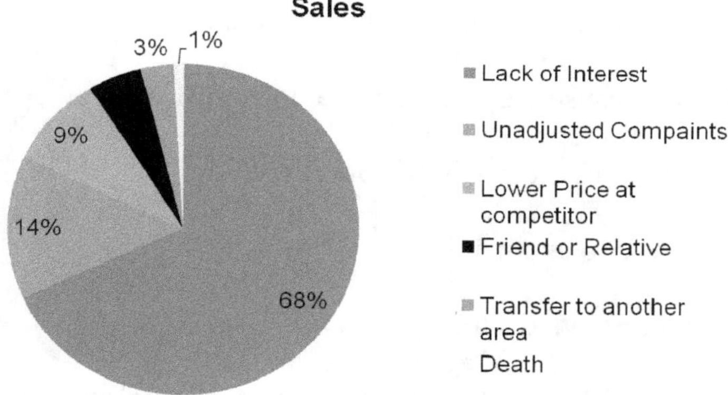

Customer Turnover Reasons

68% of the customers left because of a lack of interest on the part of the seller's employees.

14% left because of unsolved complaints.

9% left because they could buy at lower prices at other places.

5% left to buy from a friend or relative.

3% moved to another area.

1% lost through death.

Normally, the annual customer turnover should not exceed 18%. But anything beyond that should be cause for concern.

Why 18%?

If you don't have control over the price of your products, you can't stop that 9% of customers who left because they could buy at lower prices elsewhere.

Since you don't have control over the customer's choice, you can't stop that 5% of customers who want to buy from a friend or relative.

You can't stop that 3% of customers who moved to some other area.

And, of course, you don't have control over your customer's death.

BUT…

You have full control over stopping that **68%** of the customers who left because of a lack of concern on the part of the seller's employees.

Also, you have full control over stopping **14%** of customers who left because of unadjusted complaints.

So, you need to warn your staff that if they don't behave properly with customers… don't listen to customers' complaints… don't solve customers' problems… don't show interest in customers post-sales… then be ready to see 82% customer turnover in the future which they could have stopped.

Checklist to Go Through While Closing The Sales

1. Are you in a positive state of mind?

   O Yes   O No

2. Are you sure about what your prospect exactly wants?

   O Yes   O No

3. Is your prospect influenced by you/your brand reputation/your products & services/your staff?

   O Yes   O No

4. Are you sure your prospect has completely understood your offer?

   O Yes   O No

5. Is your prospect thoroughly convinced by your sales presentation?

   O Yes   O No

6. Have you answered all the queries of your prospect to their full satisfaction?

O Yes   O No

7. Does your prospect have any unspoken objections?

O Yes   O No

8. Does your prospect trust you and your company?

O Yes   O No

9. Have you noticed any buying signals from your prospect?

O Yes   O No

10. Does your prospect clearly distinguish you from your competitors?

O Yes   O No

11. Is there any reason due to which your prospect may procrastinate the buying decision?

O Yes   O No

12. Are you prepared to tackle the prospect's reason for procrastination with your reason why your prospect should buy today?

O Yes   O No

Part Three: Final Words

Why Your Customers Should Say THANKS to You?

As you have seen, generally, salespeople say Thanks to the customer after the transaction.

But do you really think that you being a salesperson should say thanks to customers for giving an order?

Well, I don't think so.

In fact, I think your customer should say Thanks to YOU for selling her a great product.

Why?

To answer this, first, let me ask you some questions...

Since how long have you been selling a product which you think is exceptionally good?

1 year?

2 years?

5 years?

20 years?

Do you still have the money you earned in all these years being a salesperson?

Are your customers still using the products that you sold over the years ago?

Now, what do you think, who is the biggest winner?

Is it you who earned some commission by selling your product at that time? I assume you might have already spent that money.

 OR

Is it your customer who is still enjoying the benefits of what you sold to her years back?

So, who do you think makes the best deal?

Of course, your customer!

Therefore, could you think again, who should say THANKS to whom after closing the deal?

Who is The #1 Enemy of A Salesperson?

When I was selling softwares at the beginning of my sales career, I attended one sales training.

The trainer asked the participants, "Who do you think is your biggest enemy?"

For a few seconds, there was a deep silence in the entire class.

And then answers started coming one by one.

One participant said: "High price."

The second participant said: "A skeptical or uneducated customer."

The third said: "Low-quality products and poor service."

Even one said: "the customer's wife."

And like these, there were a bunch of answers in the next 5-10 minutes.

After listening to all these answers carefully, the trainer gave his opinion.

He said: "I think it's the Internet."

You see, in the last 2 decades, the Internet has started eating a salesperson's job.

Many things are sold online, without any salesperson's help.

Online retail is a perfect example.

Even high-ticket items can be sold online if your website and sales page are effective.

There are many advantages to selling on the Internet.

The Internet is open 24 hours, unlike a retail shop.

The Internet works 365 days without taking any sick leaves.

The Internet doesn't have an attitude problem.

People can buy from any part of the world.

The Internet is transparent.

But have you ever wondered if the internet is so good, then why companies still hire salespeople?

Well, I think, being a salesperson, you play the role of a consultant while dealing with customers.

You listen to your customer's problems, objections, requirements; and provide the best solution to them.

In short, humans know best how to deal with humans.

Are You Ready to Challenge Your Superiors?

One of my favourite topics of discussion is incompetence.

My close associates know how much I hate incompetence.

In fact, a few years back, I developed my own theory of the entire process of an Incompetent system.

Incompetence leads to Insecurity.

Insecurity leads to Politics.

And Politics leads to an Incompetent system.

Let me explain this whole process with an example...

Suppose you're just an average salesperson in your company but quite relaxed because your job is safe.

 Maybe because you're a senior in the company.

Or maybe you have a good bonding with your boss.

Or maybe the company doesn't have any other choice at present.

But one day, the company decides to hire another sales guy who is smart, intelligent, hard worker.

Gradually this newly joined starts getting more orders than you. The whole office starts appreciating him. Calling him Go-Getter... Closer... Star Salesman.

Now tell me frankly... what is going inside your mind?

Haven't you started feeling insecure? Because you know he is a better performer and maybe one day eats your job.

Now you have two choices.

Either to grow yourself, do hard work, and become competent.

Or to throw him out of your company by playing office politics. You can involve other incompetent colleagues with you.

What do you think is an easier one for you?

Gotcha!

Don't take it personally. This is just an example to show what happens generally in offices, which are shamelessly following an incompetent system.

The point is... It's not wrong being incompetent. **The problem is making the wrong choice.**

If you make the right choice of growing yourself no matter how much time it takes, no matter how much effort it takes...

not only you'll become better in your craft, but you'll start challenging your superiors.

Trust me; it will become fun for you.

So, are you ready to challenge your seniors?

About The Author

Vibhor Asri started his career as an engineer working in software support. His job was to give demonstrations and trainings on CAD softwares.

But one day, one of Vibhor's colleagues, who was in Sales, left the company. And Vibhor was asked to handle the selling part for a few days till they get a new salesperson. Since then, he has never got a chance to leave the sales.

It was a roller-coaster ride for him, with many ups and downs. But one thing Vibhor knew right from the beginning. The top salespeople are doing something different from the rest of the mediocre salespeople.

To find out what it is, and then to learn, practice, apply, and teach became the mission of his life.

Vibhor was curious to know…

Why top 20% of salespeople make 80% of the money?

What they do differently from others?

Why they sell more than others?

Why customers buy again and again from them?

During the research, Vibhor found there are many big and small reasons because of which the top salespeople outperform others. But the most important secret he learned was that all these great salespeople are Master Persuaders.

So, it became his mission to learn, practice, apply, and even teach Persuasion.

Vibhor got recognition because of his *Persuasion Mastery Workshops*, which brought a revolution in the sales training industry. Persuasion is more than a passion for him. It changed his life completely.

For the last 15 years, Vibhor is studying and practicing Persuasion.

And now it's your turn.

In his course *Becoming A Master of Closing Sales*, Vibhor shared many secrets, thought processes, habits, and techniques of the top 20% Master Salespeople, which help them in closing more and more deals every day.

Vibhor writes a monthly newsletter, *Persuade and Grow Rich*, in which he shares principles and techniques of Persuasion along with their applications. To know more about his newsletter and other courses, visit his website www.vibhorasri.com

On his website, you'll also find hundreds of blogs and sales tips shared by Vibhor regularly.

Digital Courses

Become A Master of Closing Sales: The ultimate course on Closing Deals

Decoding Your Customer's Mind: Why your customer chooses you over your competitors?

Persuade and Grow Rich: A streetsmart for small businesses to convert NOs into YESes

Turn Your Business into Cashflow Machine: A proven automatic method to bring new customers and repeated sales from existing customers

LIVE Online Trainings

Types of Trainings

Public Workshop

In-house Training

One-to-One Coaching

Topics

Mastering Persuasion in Business: Learn science & art of persuasion in converting NOs into YESes

Become A Master of Closing Deals: Learn how to deal with objections and the most powerful closing techniques

www.vibhorasri.com

Notes

Notes

Notes

Notes